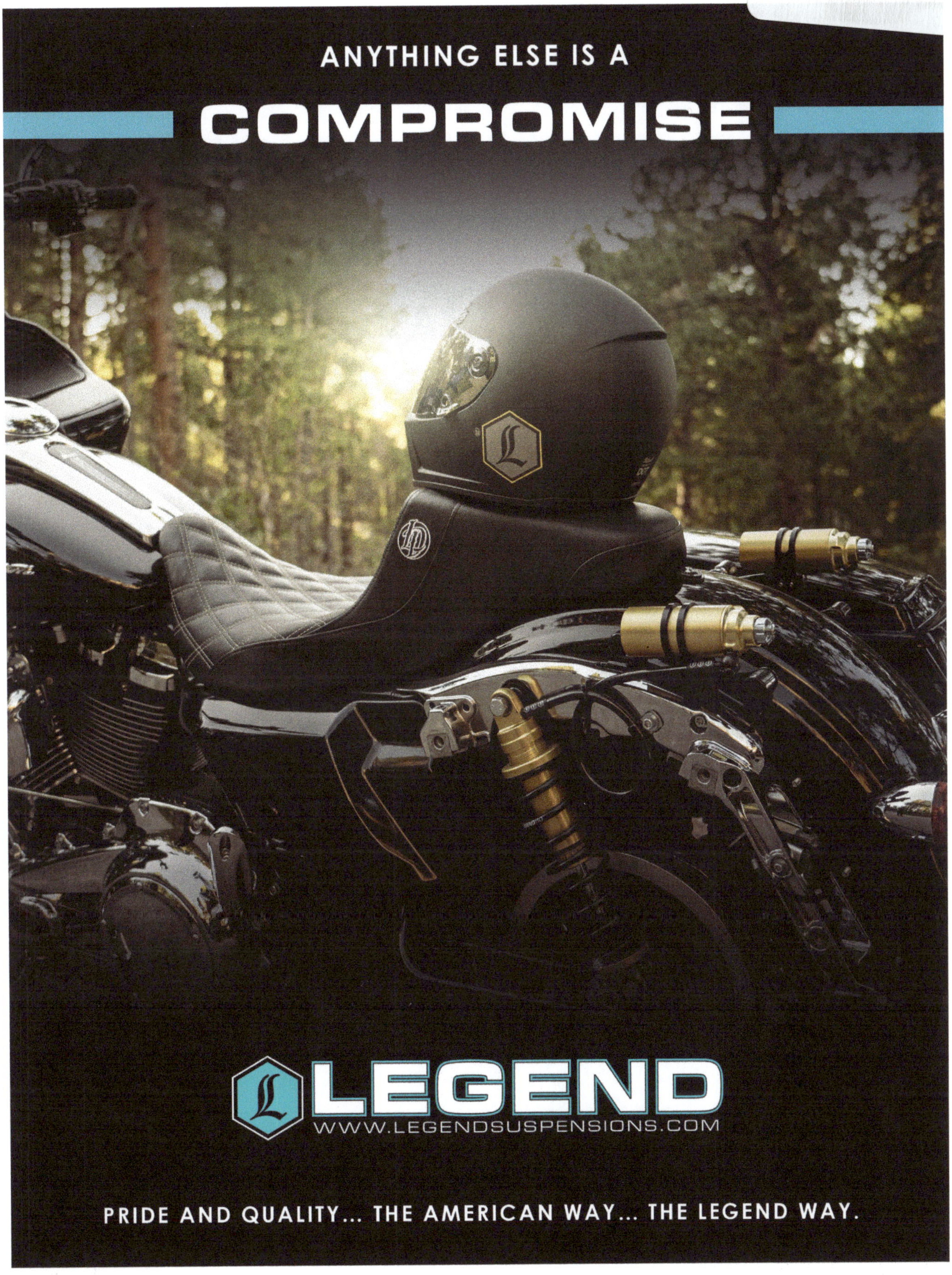
ANYTHING ELSE IS A
COMPROMISE
LEGEND
WWW.LEGENDSUSPENSIONS.COM
PRIDE AND QUALITY... THE AMERICAN WAY... THE LEGEND WAY.

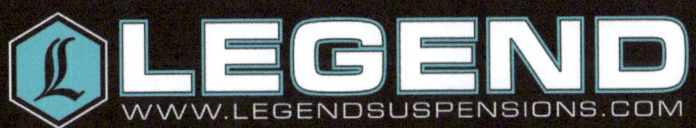

Harley-Davidson Performance Bagger

By Timothy Remus

Published by:
Wolfgang Publication Inc.
P.O. Box 223
Stillwater, MN 55082

ISBN: 978-1-941064-71-9
Printed in USA

THE PERFECT COMBINATION

BST Carbon Fiber Wheels

- 40-60% weight savings vs. OEM
- Unparalleled aesthetic upgrade
- Direct OEM replacement
- Quicker acceleration and reduced braking distance
- Reduces rider fatigue

BST Wheels are the exclusive carbon fiber wheels of the BRL

West Coast Bagger Swingarm

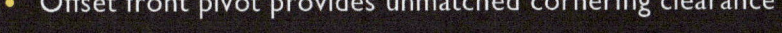

- Handcrafted 6061-T6 aluminum 0-3" extended swingarm
- Proudly designed, machined, and assembled in the USA
- 42% weight savings vs. OEM
- Features 3-position shock mounts
- Offset front pivot provides unmatched cornering clearance

Your 'go to' source for **STUPID FAST** motorcycle parts

BrocksPerformance.com
(937) 912-0054

Legals

First published in 2023 by Wolfgang Publications Inc.
P.O. Box 223
Stillwater, MN 55082

© Timothy Remus 2023

All rights reserved. With the exception of quoting brief passages for the purposes of review no part of this publication may be reproduced without prior written permission from the publisher.

The information in this book is true and complete to the best of our knowledge. All recommendations are made without any guarantee on the part of the author or publisher, who also disclaim any liability incurred in connection with the use of this data or specific details.

We recognize that some words, model names and designations, for example, mentioned herein, are the property of the trademark holder. We use them for identification purposes only. This is not an official publication.

ISBN: 978-1-941064-71-9

Table of Contents

1. History 9
2. Brakes 19
3. Suspension 26
4. Fairings and Fenders 39
5. Driveline 43
6. Crate Motors 48
7. Ward Performance 53
8. Carbon Fiber 59
9. Not John's First Bagger 68
10. The Three Baggers 74
11. Big-Wheel Softail meets Performance Bagger 84
12. Motorwitch 88
13. Trask 97
14. Randy & Joe 106
15. D&D 116
16. Pipes 118
17. Skunk on the Loose 123
18. The Power of Suggestion 127
19. More than a Performance Bagger 131
20. You have to Look Twice 136

Acknowledgements

I'm grateful to the long list of men and women who gave up time and information to help me put together this Performance Bagger book. No order here… There's a long list of bike builders, owners and individuals working in the aftermarket:

Curtis Hofmann. Kory Souza. The MotorWitch (Danny Wilson). Randy Cramer Nick Trask, and his side-kick Moots, Shadley Bros. Paul and Mark, Pipes (Pipes Gilliland), Chaz – just Chaz because his full name would take up the whole page. Tom Sperr, Paul Yaffe, Bert Baker, Brian Klock, Paul Yaffe, Rick Ward, Brian Gall and Mark Foff.

Dedication

I would like to dedicate this book to a man we all know in the flesh or by reputation - Arlen Ness.

In 1989 I was lucky enough to land a contract with Motorbooks to write a book about this bike builder named Arlen Ness. That project went well, and the book came out in early 1990. In the late summer of that year I looked Arlen up in Sturgis. And Arlen, being the gentleman he always was, introduced me to a small group of very talented bike builders from all over the country, builders like Donnie Smith, Dave Perewitz and Hotop.

Without Arlen I might never have met that group of talented builders – and never written motorcycle books for 30+ years.

– Thanks Arlen

Thanks to One and All

It's looking like this is my last book, or at least the last technical book, and I want to thank a long list of men and women who helped me create books and more books.

I have to start with the names at the top of the page and add the following: Donnie Smith, Rob Roehl, Don Tima, Skeeter Todd, Bruce Bush, Tank, Shadleys, Rodney, John Reed, Neil Ryan, Mr. Flame David, Brian Klock, Leah and Brian Gall, Reggie Jr. and Sr., Jon Kos, and Michael Urseth who did the layout on the first ten books and for teaching me how to use a camera. Credits for the pics on the back cover: Horst from Germany for the Wheelie picture, and Brian Klock for the Flag-Man. I thank the Team of Eric and Monica for the layout, and Penny for bringing in the companies from the industry.

Finally, all the name-less helpers who set a cylinder head on a cylinder three times so I can get the perfect photo, or the poor suckers who got up at 5:00 AM to help me push an 800 pound bike up a mountain as the sun is coming up. And finally the woman who proof-read at least 30 books - Mary Lanz.

photo credit: DINO PETROCELLI

A Special thanks to Tim Remus and Wolfgang Publications for your support and friendship over the past 30 years.

Mark and Paul Shadley
Shadley Bros

Introduction

How Did we Get Here - A short history

The first motorcycle that you can call a Bagger showed up in the show rooms in 1980. That new frame was longer, had a triangle under the seat, and for the first time the motor and transmission floated on rubber mounts. A big part of the vibration that riders took for granted - disappeared. That new FLT used the Shovel for power, but in two years, the Shovel was traded for the Evo.

Now, put that new motor in that new frame with the rubber mounts, and life is truly good on the road. Evos were great, but no one called those Performance Baggers. Development at Milwaukee continued and in 1999 the Twin Cam came out. Bigger and more powerful those Baggers with the early TC motors, those bikes were on their way to the Dresser with Performance.

The term, Performance Bagger, really came into use in 2017. The M-8 motors came in 107 and 114 cubic inches. More displacement is important, but what might be more important than more cubes is the fact that the new M-8 came with more valves. And four valves will pass more air (and exhaust) than two – no matter how big those two big valves are.

This book brings you a detailed look at these new Baggers. The book includes interviews and input from people like Bert Baker and Rick Ward, and techs who work for companies like Ohlins or Beringer. In addition to the techs and experts, the bulk of the pages are filled with pictures and the story of Performance Baggers. Some are Twin Cam powered and some have a M-8 under the tank. The one thing that they have in common is the fact that they all can be described as Performance Baggers.

Chapter 1

Bagger History

by Chaz

What we call Baggers started in 1980, when Harley-Davidson brought out a new bike with a new frame - the FLT. Moving from the old Shovelhead FL/FX frame to the FLT rubber-mount platform was a big step. Handling and comfort were improved, but it was a big, slow Bagger. In 1999 Harley Davidson introduced the Twin Cam and the aftermarket was on it for performance and appearance parts. Suddenly, Baggers are cool.

Road Kings, Electra Glides and Road Glides were everywhere. Custom wheels, custom paint, custom seats and hot rod motors were the order of the day.

One of the big changes for Harley came from the introduction of the Electra Glide Standard. This was an Electra Glide striped down to basics. The Motor Company marketed it as a "Sport Tourer." The excited new owner got an Electra Glide with a batwing fairing, saddlebags and the new Twin Cam

Two very clean Baggers, both the ownership of the Shadley Bros.
This fine example is a 1980 FLHT first-year, with original paint that still shines.

The early bags look a little crude, just give the designers a few years.

From the basic shape of the bags is already there, essentially the same shape we have today. Along with that over-stuffed seat for two.

some who continued to work to build what we would eventually call the Performance Bagger.

There are a few motorcycles which really set the pace for this movement. The first one was built by Brian Klock and Klock Werks in Mitchell, South Dakota. The Klock Werks Team captured the imagination of FLT riders worldwide when they ran the "World's Fastest Bagger" at Bonneville and set a world record. People wanted to know everything about it. How it was built, could it be ridden on the street, and could they get one or build one? The specs for the bike were fairly simple, but the work was not. The bike was built on a custom Rolling Thunder chassis with Works Performance shocks and Race Tech fork internals. The motor, a S&S 124 pushing 173 HP was mated to a Baker 6 speed transmission. BST Carbon fiber wheels were adapted, and the Harley body work was lightened. The motorcycle set records in 2006, 2007 and 2008 with a top speed of 161 MPH. Now fast Baggers were cool.

In 2009 made the next big modification to the FLT frame. The frame was lengthened and now had a 180mm rear tire. Other changes were an improved front fork, a low-profile front tire to work with the new rear and a 96 CI motor with a 6-speed transmission. The new Screaming Eagle overbore kit was 103 cubic inch and the CVO models had the 110 cubic inch motor. The 103 cubic inch motor would become the standard in a couple of years. In 2014 the Rushmore models came with a new fork assembly. The tubes measured 49mm, and both triple trees had a good grip on those big tubes. These improvements were welcomed by enthusiasts. However, more and more builders were producing "big wheel Bagger" show bikes, and fewer and fewer were working on the performance end of the spectrum.

In many ways the evolution of the Performance Bagger seemed to have stopped. Suspension manufacturers worked on building air suspensions for show bikes. Speed and performance manufacturers are always looking to get more out of a motor but, body components such as fairings, saddlebags and side covers were becoming heavier and more ornate. Exhausts became heavier because they are being hidden under the saddlebags. The big wheels were getting bigger, everything was longer without purpose. While it seemed function over form had been thrown out the window, there were some beacons of hope, and they came from an unlikely source.

In 2014, Harley Davidson introduced the Rushmore line of FLTs. The new Road King, Street Glide and Electra Glide models were hitting the floor. The Road Glide wouldn't be released until the following model year due to a new fairing design. These bikes were popular. The Rushmore 103 CI motor offered improved performance, the new "Infotainment System" provided navigation, music, phone and MP3 connectivity and the suspension was improved. The CVO bikes were still equipped with the 110 CI motor, but anyone could buy a Screaming Eagle 120 R motor and have it installed in their new bike with a factory warranty. The bikes were a hit with the riding public. Performance equipment manufacturers expanded their product lines around the new

A good look at the Shovelhead, and note how the front exhaust pipe winds around the cylinder and runs down the left side, not the way the exhaust is routed today.

The Shovelhead displaces 80 cubic inches, the transmission is a five-speed unit. The shaped gas tank holds five gallons of ethel. Not the fastest V-twin, but a better motor is around the corner.

The Shovel went away and the Evo took it's place, as you can see in this very nice example of a 1998 Bagger. It's trully an original bike, right down to the mufflers and pipes.

The Evo routes both pipes on the right side to the split behind the rear cylinder. Note the anniversary badge on the tank – yes - Harley-Davidson survived bad times and prosperous times for 95 years.

offerings from the Motor Company. One of these new products came from S&S and it made a big statement.

In 2014 S&S released the Dragon 143. A bolt-in 143 CI monster motor producing 160 HP and 170 FT LB torque for $10,000.00. Then S&S put it in a bike for everyone to see. The bike was built using parts commonly available to everyone and every part had a specific purpose. The 143 Dragon being the heart of the motorcycle, other parts were BST carbon fiber wheels from Brock's Performance, 13-inch Lydall rotors, Ohlins suspension and a host of other performance parts. The bike was advertised as a daily rider and was even ridden to Sturgis in 2015. It still makes appearances at drag strips all over the Mid-West. Enthusiasts liked this bike - they wanted one.

The next big jump in the evolution of the Performance Bagger came with the introduction of the M-8 motors in 2017. Here's a motor that comes in three displacements: 107, 114 and 117 cubic inches. Better yet, add a big bore kit, and these motors jump to 124, 128, and 131 inches.

When compared with the Twin Cam, the M-8 offers more than cubic inches. To simplify; four small valves have more area than two big ones. Porting shops and specialists found out that with a mild porting job, the M-8 flows roughly 50% more air than a Twin Cam with a similar porting job.

The 1998 FHLT looks pretty modern for the day.
The name Evo is the appropriate name for the motor – and the Baggers as well.

Add a good camshaft, two-into-one exhaust, air filter and a dyno run, you have a very streetable motor that's putting out an easy 150 or 160 horses – and there's more readily available. Now the word Performance really fits the description of these very fast motorcycles.

Lately custom builders and manufactures have started to push towards the Performance Bagger genre of building. Race Tech, Legends and Ohlins are building the performance suspensions to make these bikes handle better. Many suspension products are designed to increase ground clearance to improve lean angle. Brock's Performance, Trask Performance and others are building swingarms to help keep the power on the ground and to keep the bikes stable at speed. Carbon fiber wheels are now available from Brock's Performance to fit almost any application. Many wheel manufacturers are building wheels for front wide tires such as 180/18 or 180/21. Custom Fabricators like Hoffman Designs and SBC Performance are building carbon fiber body parts for Harleys and Indians. S&S makes everything one could want to put in a motor and Trask Performance will put a turbo on it.

So, what is a "Performance Bagger"? Owners are building Performance Baggers to use day to day. The most common modifications are motor, suspension, weight and appearance. The key ingredients or modifications are usually tailored to the individual owners' tastes and of course pocketbook. Motor modifications go anywhere from an exhaust system to complete high performance rebuilds and crate

The Evo motor, in place of the Shovels, was a big launch forward for Harley-Davidson. Eighty cubic inches of a modern motor with new aluminum cylinders with steel liners, and a modern cylinder head, also aluminum. Now all the major components were aluminum, so there's fewer leaks and more power. Next came the Twin Cam Baggers, and no one called them "performance" bikes, but there were builders like Brian Klock who took those machines to the Salt and broke all kinds of records. And the next generation broke those records and a hundred more. Well done Harley-Davidson.

motors. Suspension modifications start at shock replacements and go to exotic Ohlin's inverted systems. Owners are shaving weight anywhere it is practical. Lithium batteries, Carbon Fiber body parts and wheels are more and more common. Seats are designed not only for comfort but to enhance rider performance. Handlebars are setup to improve rider control and maneuvering. The performance Bagger movement has been a slow-moving evolution based on owners desires to gain more power, handling and style from these heavy bikes.

As more and more Baggers are being built like this bike, the next step was inevitable. Enter MotoAmerica's King of the Baggers race and The Bagger Racing League. See the story from Eric Herrmann.

What we have today, are bikes with the speed and handling of the Kawasaki Ninja and Hyabusa from Suzuki, but with the comforts and saddle bags you can find only on a Bagger from Harley-Davidson and Indian.

As Joe Duenser said: Hot rod Baggers are in my blood. I like the long-distance capabilities of the Baggers, but I also have to have the performance.

Photos by Shadleys

Bagger Racing

by Eric Herrmann

With the popularity of Baggers increasing over the last decade, Bagger racing is nothing new. The availability of performance and suspension components has spearheaded the racing aspect of these once considered "Geezer Glides". Overweight touring bikes can now be transformed into formidable race bikes.

Any form of racing advances the technology of the equipment. Motors, Suspension, lightweight Carbon Fiber parts, Racing Controls, have all been developed due to these racing efforts. Thanks to an aftermarket industry, this racing R&D has developed race proven parts that are now available to the average Bagger rider.

Since the early 2000's The Bub Motorcycle Speed trials held annually at Bonneville has had a class for "The Worlds Fastest Bagger". Top speeds have escalated over the years from 140mph to 240mph. Notable industry professionals such as Brian Klock and Chris Rivas, amongst others, have created products to advance this segment of Land Speed Racing.

Drag Racing has had a Pro Bagger Class for many years now. The speeds and times have improved significantly, and we now have 7 second quarter mile Baggers. Once again, this improvement in equipment and technology is mainly due to passionate individuals involved in the sport.

Rob Buydos created Bagger Racing and the Bagger Racing League with a goal of going to Daytona!

The Trask Turbo in hot pursuit!

Bagger racer Danny Eslick on the charge!

My Garage Ventura on the gas at a Bagger Racing League Race

This brings us to the latest Racing development, Bagger Road Racing. Rob Buydos, well known Motorsport Announcer, noticed the trend towards Performance Baggers, and thought it would be interesting to put on an Exhibition Road Race with Performance Baggers. The first "King of the Baggers" race was held at Laguna Seca raceway in October of 2020. This exhibition race was hosted by Moto America in conjunction with their popular Sport Bike Racing series. The Race was won by Tyler O'Hara on an Indian Challenger and re-sparked a 100-year-old rivalry between Indian Motorcycle and Harley-Davidson.

The popularity of this race exceeded the interest in the Sport Bike Races! Bagger Racing reached hundreds of thousands through live and streaming TV. Bagger Road Racing was off to a great start.

Moto America continued the "King of the Bagger" race series with several races throughout the country the following years. These races are held in conjunction with their Sport Bike Racing series. The television audience has grown and major sponsors from outside the Motorcycle Industry have stepped up to support the sport and get their products noticed.

Rob had a different vision and created "The Bagger Racing League." His concept was to hold races specifically for American V-Twins. Harley's and Indians. While there are several different classes, Bagger GP, Pro-Stock Bagger, Light Weight Twins... they are all American V-Twins. If you're fortunate enough to attend a race, you won't watch sport bikes race all day waiting for The Bagger Race at the end of the day. It will be nonstop racing on loud, fast, American Bikes! The Bagger Racing League has also made racing accessible to the public. With a few short classes you can acquire a race license and bring your bike to the track. We love the Privateers and the ability to come and race your own bike. While there is factory Indian and Harley- Davidson teams I enjoy the racing efforts of my friends at smaller companies. Trask Performance, Saddlemen, Barnett Clutches, Performance Machine, are involved in Bagger Racing. Their knowledge learned at the Track will translate into better equipment for your Bagger. Support those who support the Sport!

Bagger Racing League Champion Belts being handed out on the Winner's Circle Podium.

The vibe at these races makes them worth attending. Most tracks have camping in or near the pit area. Racers are prepping bikes, barbequing, and doing dumb stuff on pit bikes. Stunt shows are held on Harleys & Indians, and custom bike shows are part of the excitement. It's like Sturgis at a Race Track. Fun to watch on TV, but way better to spend a weekend at the Track if they come near your town. As this series grows, I'm sure more Industry vendors will bring bikes and products to display and purchase.

Now to address the naysayers. Why not have BMW's or Goldwings? They're not American V-Twins! If you've heard 20 Performance V-Twins thundering around the track, you'd understand.

These bikes are extremely fast with professional riders. I compare it to the difference between F-1 racing or NASCAR. F-1 are faster and more technologically advanced, but the loud, brashness of NASCAR is more appealing to the general public.

Bagger Racing is a sight to see! The riding skills these racers have to muscle a 600 pound bike through tight corners is amazing. Pushing big Horsepower and no traction control, they wheelie off the line as they slam into the first corner. So if you say, why race Baggers, go to a Race! You'll understand why they aren't racing BMW's and Goldwings. Whatever series you choose to follow, King of the Baggers, or The Bagger Racing League, you're in for an exciting weekend!

Chapter 2
Brakes - Basics & Physics

Before talking about breaking components, we need to talk about the layout, and some of the basic physics that are involved. Brakes are basically hydraulic; the master cylinder pushes fluid under pressure through the hoses down to the calipers. Fluids can't be compressed – so pressure on one end of a hose is the same at the other end.

Given two master cylinders from the same manufacturer and squeezed by the same person with the same power and stroke, the master cylinder with the smaller piston (diameter) will have more pressure and less volume.

The cylinder works the other way around. Two calipers, one with larger pistons (area) and one smaller, 100 psi is applied to both. And the caliper with the larger pistons area will have more force on the pads and require more volume of brake fluid.

The whole idea of this little discussion is to make readers understand that a master cylinder

For his fresh Performance Bagger, John Jessup mounted two four-piston calipers in the radial mounts in the lower leg. All the parts, including the rotors, carry the Ness logo.

Pipes chose two, four-piston calipers, mounted in the standard way, and mated to a pair of modern rotors.

Seen in one of the race Baggers, a complete master cylinder from Beringer.

Some builders and owners retain the factory caliper on the back. Motorwitch used a radial mount in the back of the stripped down Bagger.

needs to be matched with the caliper(s). You can get more pressure with a certain master cylinder, but you may not have enough volume to the calipers when the Buick stops right in stop of you.

Here's an example of how a professional bike builder like Randy Cramer from Dakota V-twin picks brake components: "Both Brembo and Beringer have the same size and number of caliper pistons so if I switch the calipers from Brembo to Beringer I don't have to change the master cylinder with a different diameter (I may change to a Beringer master cylinder just because it's a very good master). Either caliper brand works good with the pressure and volume of the Beringer Master Cylinder. If I do have any questions about what works with what I ask the staff at Kraus Moto, and they suggest components and usually have the components in stock. Hope this helps."

Calipers

Brake calipers come with everything from one to six pistons. In the case of late model Baggers we're going to talk about (mostly) 4-piston calipers. The Twin Cam Baggers came with four-piston calipers up front, and they're way better than the calipers they replaced. Better four-piston calipers were installed on Baggers starting 1999, and they're still four-piston calipers.

A somewhat late entry to the high-end aftermarket brakes market, Beringer, is a company that got their start manufacturing brake components for aircraft. Today, Beringer makes high quality braking components for aircraft, automobiles, Quads and of course, motorcycles – both competition bikes as well as for high performance street machines – like Sport Bikes and Performance Baggers. The following Q&A is from Philippe Danh from Beringer.

Is a six-piston caliper a "better caliper" for a high performance motorcycle, than a four-piston caliper? Stubby/blocky 4-piston radial mount calipers tend to have a more abrupt initial bite because they are very rigid and flex-less, open-up less under very hard braking pressures

(350 psi +). Six-piston axial caliper are just as powerful, offer the same ultimate clamping force but offer a tiny bit of flex which translates into more braking comfort. This is why 90% of Supermoto race bikes run Beringer's six-piston caliper rather than four-piston radial calipers.

Why has the high performance brake market switched to radial-mount calipers on the fork? Your questions are simple, but necessitate a lengthy reply because several factors are involved in the switch from axial mount calipers to radial mount calipers in the early 2000s. There is more than technicity here. There is also production factors and fashion/trendiness/perceived performance.

One big factor for people and race shops to switch from axial mount calipers to radial calipers is practicality. Radial calipers can be moved up and down on the fork mount, via spacers, to accommodate different size rotors. You cannot do that with axial mount calipers. With axial mounts you are stuck with one size rotors and that's it.

On the manufacturing/OEM level, it is much easier for the manufacturers of forks like Showa, Kayaba, Ohlins and others, to offer one single caliper mount

Beringer four-piston calipers, mounted in a radial mount and floating rotors.

A Ness test bike with their pair of their calipers and ventilated rotors.

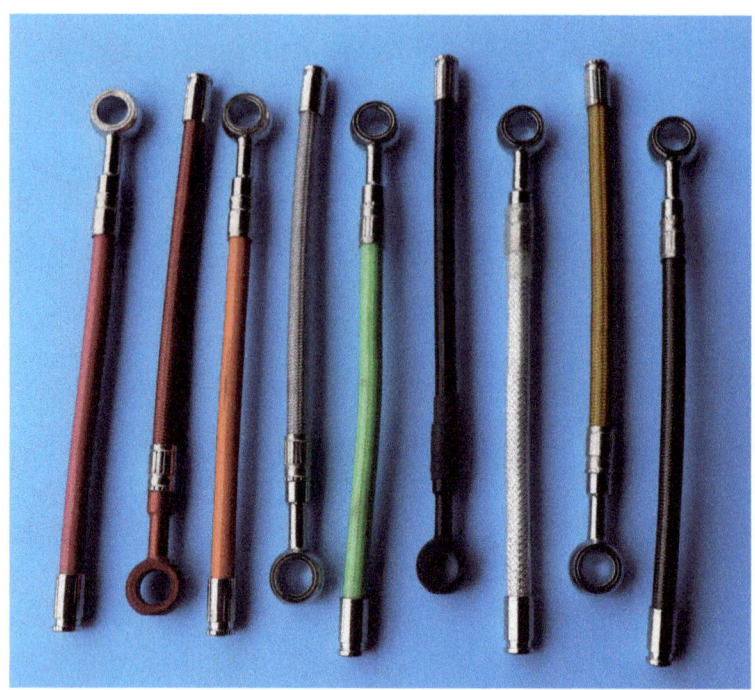

Galfer, known for rotors, also makes its own lines with Dupont Teflon carrier the juice, protected by the stainless and PVC coating. Obvious, llines are purchased in colors that can likely match your bike.

A Ness six-piston caliper, with pistons of gradual diameters.

(radial 4-piston) and spacers of different heights to accommodate various size rotors. In the past, fork manufacturers had to offer many different fork legs with caliper mounts higher or lower, with different bolt spreads etc.

Radial mount calipers come in only 2 mounting bolt spreads: 100mm and 108mm and you need a right and left side. That's only four-calipers to make. As opposed to perhaps 30-40 different axial calipers. It is generally accepted that 100mm calipers are offered on medium performance street bikes and lower displacement sportbikes. The 108mm bolt spread radial calipers are mounting on all the big bore sport bikes, Superbike and Moto GP race bikes.

And now, radial mount is associated with racing and high performance, and Bagger owners see the race bikes and want them on their bikes - even though Beringer's direct bolt-on 6-piston axial mount calipers would offer nearly identical performance to the stock brakes. It's a matter of perception by the public.

Radial mount calipers made everybody's life easier.

Rotors

Not so long ago, for regular riders, rotors were rotors. What came with the bike was good enough. Polished, perfectly round discs with some holes was good enough. The only ones who really gave a damn were the competition riders, and the riders who built their bike from scratch, then there were thoughts about which calipers, pads and which rotors to mate with the caliper.

Today, for the Performance Bagger gang, everything relating to braking is under close examination. And one of those items is the rotors. Today, the rotors look like a mistake, a F-up. For an explanation of those new rotors with random holes with funny shapes, and an outside edge that's anything but round – we have Mark Crookston long-time employee of Galfer, a somewhat new to the Harley and Performance Bagger markets.

Why the wave rotors, why not plain old round rotors? Better tooling. Lighter weight.

Wave is designed to create vortexes to pull heat off the rotor. Our Wave® pattern takes that leading edge of contact between the blade and pad and constantly move it up and down, thus minimizing heat build-up. Cool air is also introduced in greater amounts.

Are all your rotors made from stainless steel? Yes, they're made from 420 hi-carbon - medical high carbon. Our propriety material is able to withstand the heat, and our rotors don't warp. We use that same stainless for all our rotors, we buy sheets of the material and cut out our shapes and sizes.

Another four-piston caliper from Beringer with a radial style mount. Note the spacers between the mount and the caliper, to position the caliper correctly.

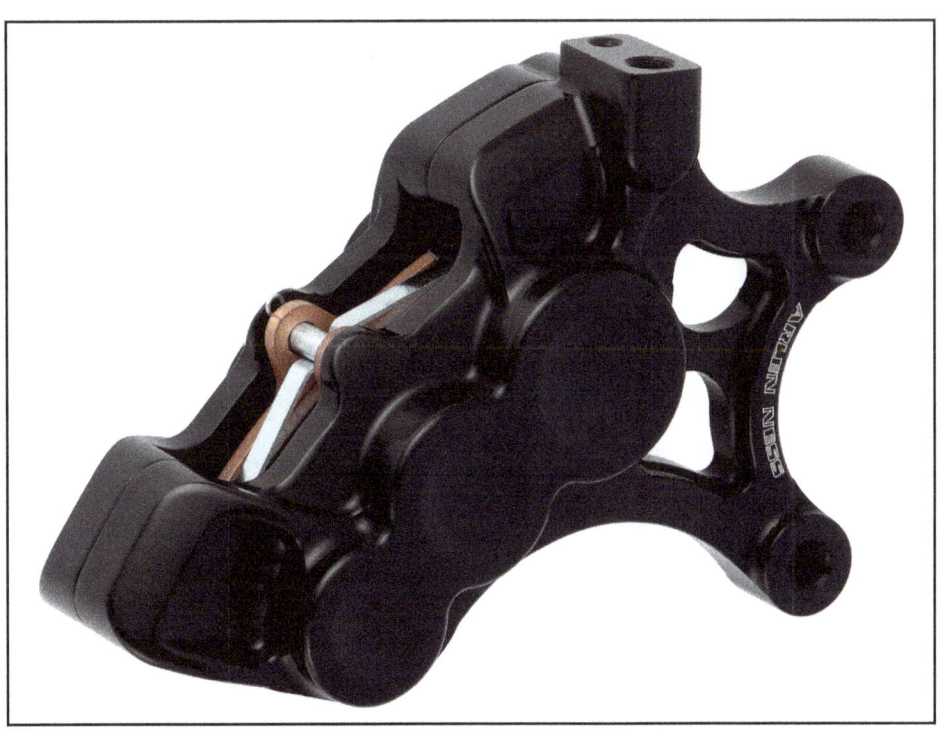

Three-piston, with gradual pistons, set up for a front end.

Mark Crookston from Gafler is one man who believes in his products – because he's part of the family that founded the company in 1952.

What are the advantages of floating rotors vs one-piece rotors? Well first, the hub of some wheels are designed such that they simply can't accept a floating rotor. But a floating rotor allows pads to always maintain full contact with the rotor under braking forces. The feel is different.

What is the center component made from the floating rotors? Our hubs for the floating rotors are cut from 7071 aluminum, it's a step up from the more common 6061 series aluminum.

What materials are your pads made of, what are the options? Galfer offers various materials, but for V-Twin, Baggers, we mostly

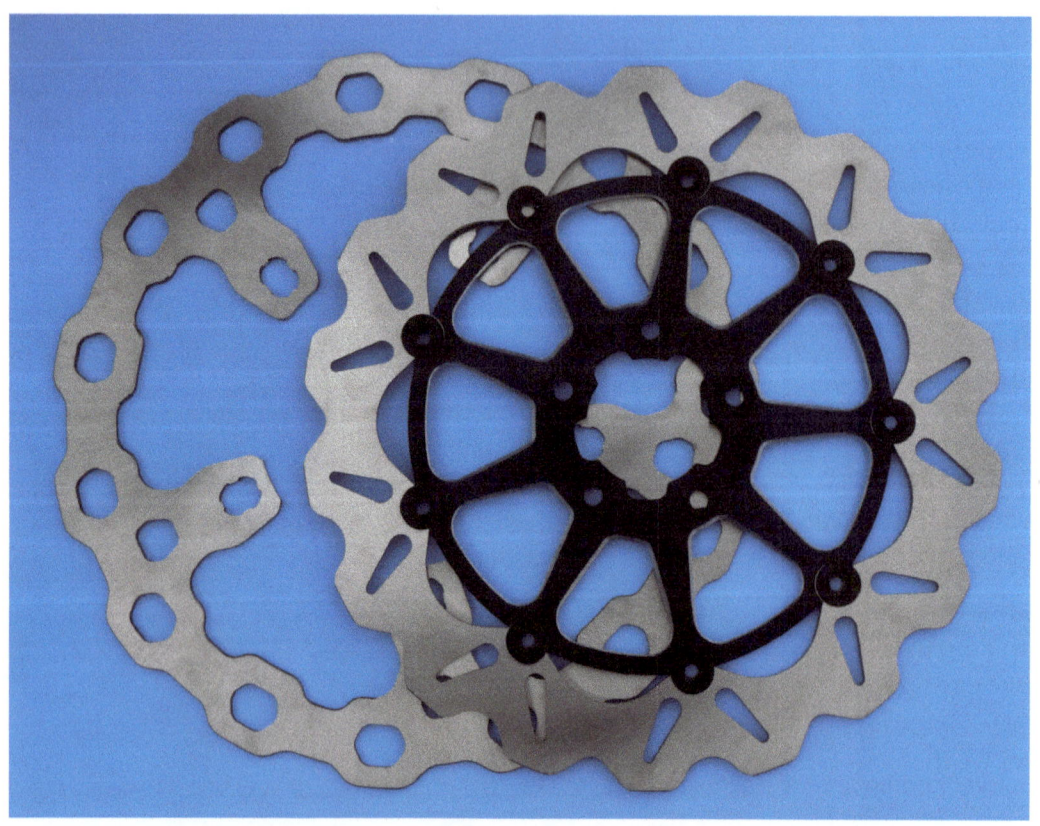

Rotors from Galfer, all are cut from high quality stainless. Note the rotor with a hub, and the other rotor without a bub, designed to bolt right to most of the current H-D wheels.

recommend HH sintered pads, because they withstand the high heat of heavy bikes. We also like the sintered pads because they offer a strong initial bite, and all through the braking process.

What about lines. Stainless Steel vs. Nylon or Rubber line? We make our own lines, and start with Dupont Teflon for the inner hose, wrapped in stainless braid, and then coated with a PVC coating. Our premium-colored ends are aluminum.

Final advice? If there is one item you can add that will make an instant, noticeable improvement to your brake feel and performance, switching to stainless steel braided line is the one!

Above: When you really have to slow down, the Sintered brake pads grab right NOW – once you go from some other material, to sintered, you will never go back.

Below: Manufactured for Trask, the front calipers are four-piston designs.

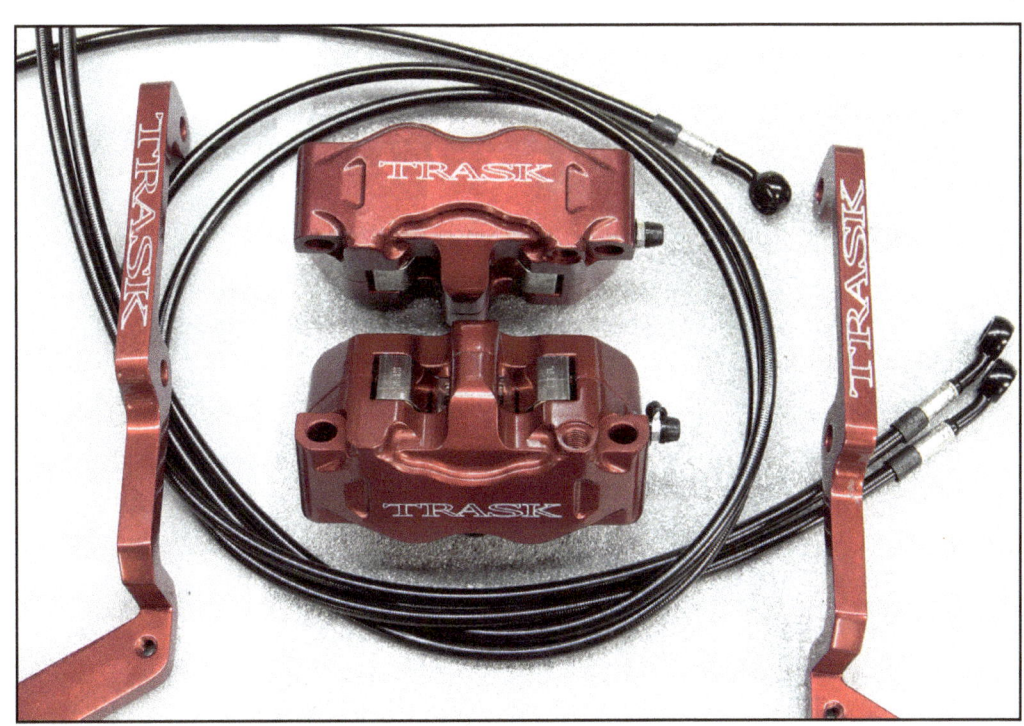

Chapter 3

Suspension

For motorcycles, what we call a shock is actually a spring and shock absorber in one structure (and in fact, the fork legs are like a shock absorber, the tube includes a spring and means of damping those springs). What follows is a primarily discussion about the shock absorber.

Suspension is what keeps your wheels on the road, especially when you're moving over bumps or hauling through a corner. There's two primary parts to the suspension, the spring and the damper. Without the damper, the bike that goes over a bump goes up and down and up and down again and again. The shocks damp the cycles of the spring. A simple damper is a tubular shock filled with oil and a piston that passes through that oil as the wheel goes up and down.

When you're hauling ass through a curve, or a series of curves, you really do need the best suspension components.

Simple shocks have two valves located on the piston, held closed by small springs. One opens on compression and the other opens when the shock extends (rebound). Obviously, as the quality and price of the shock go up, the simple shock become a very sophisticated combination of spring and damper. The valves become much more sophistication, and both the rebound the compression mechanism are adjustable.

A bumpy road will have the piston going up and down so fast that the oil gets very hot and the oil is aerated. Aerated oil won't damp the motion of the piston. The solution of better shocks has the chamber of gas under pressure which pressures the oil inside the shock and minimizes the aerating. The downside of having the gas chamber inside the shock is the fact that the chamber reduces the space for oil. So, the really expensive shocks use a remote gas pressure chamber. These shocks are likely to have adjustments for rebound, and compression.

Forks

Like shocks, forks have springs and a damper mechanism much like shocks.

There are only two types or forks on Baggers, the conventional fork assembly with the small diameter leg bolted into the triple trees, and the wheel is mounted to the larger diameter component that slides up and down.

The more modern fork aftermarket assembly flips the

Top: From Ness, kits that include 49mm tubes (in black of gold finish, stock or 2 inches longer) and the ribbed lower legs with a connecting link, and 4-piston calipers and an axle. Fits 17 and up Touring bikes.

Right: A variety of handlebars and risers makes it easy to modify your Bagger to a better fit and a cleaner look. Ness

Legend's remote reservoir shocks, available for Baggers from 2009 to the current models. Yours can be 13 or 14 inches long, and available black or gold. All the adjustments can be done without any tools.

In 2014 H-D introduced a much better fork assembly – 49 mm legs and a much better triple trees. Now there are kits shown with the 'trees and complete legs that can work on earlier Baggers. In most cases the original wheel, calipers and the axle will work. You may need new hoses. Neil Ryan, MPLS.

Two Brembo calipers, mounted in a radial style – squeezing ventilated rotors bolted to a Brock's Carbon Fiber wheel.

two major components (often called inverted) the larger diameter component is bolted into the trees, and the smaller diameter component is the lower component that supports the axle and the calipers.

You might say, "why swap the two components?"

The larger and stronger of the two major components are in the triple trees. By making the smaller tube the one that goes up and down, you reduce the unsprung weight.

Unsprung weight: Moves up and down with the wheels as they travel over bumps, potholes, and other obstructions. So unsprung weight includes (for the front of a motorcycle): the lowest tube of the fork assemblies, wheels, tires, brake assemblies, and anything directly connected to the wheels.

For the 2014, Baggers received higher quality forks. The "new" fork is better and stronger in a number of ways. Though the fork legs are traditional (not inverted), they are considerably larger and stronger than the fork legs that proceeded. Another great improvement is the triple trees, both the upper and lower tree are beefy, and both grab the tubes with a heavy clamp.

For bikes manufactured before 2014, there are kits from companies like Race Tech and Legend. They provide kits that include a set of more sophisticated valves, and most of companies also offer cartridges that replace everything inside the tubes. In fact, some stock pre-2014 Baggers came with cartridges in the forks.

Given the fact that 2014 and later forks are better than the ones H-D replaced, clever motor-heads have found a way to install those new forks on older chassis. One of those motor-heads is Neil Ryan who provides two legs with new guts, and new triple trees. Note the photo nearby.

The difference between what we call Performance Bagger, and a Bagger with a Blower or Turbo or big-ass motor is the fact that true Performance Bagger includes the whole machine. You don't have to buy the very best components, but you can't just skip the suspension and brakes. Big power means more speed. You will encounter speed when the light suddenly turns red, and when you lean into a tight turn at a speed faster than your normal pace. Be good to that machine, it's your partner when you're on the street. Take pride of your machine and that machine will do its best to take care of you.

An Ohlins Cartidge with nice features: compression damping in the left leg and rebound damping in the right. Adjustments are made at the top with the spring preload. The cartridge system fits bolt-on and are easy to install in standard front forks.

If you want a more aggressive sitting position, throw away those floorboards that old geezers use. Install these mid-controls in the same frame mounts. Arms are made from aluminum; floor pegs are not included. Ness

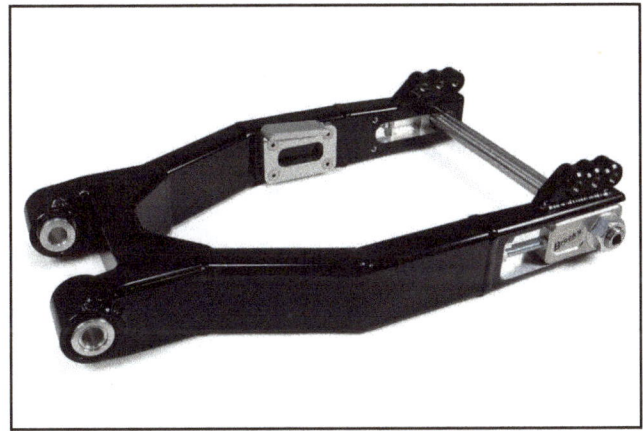

A Swingarm from Brock's, aluminum and designed to be both stronger and lighter as the stock component. Wheel position can be stock or up to 3 inches back. Wider or stock wheels and tires, comes with spherical bearings.

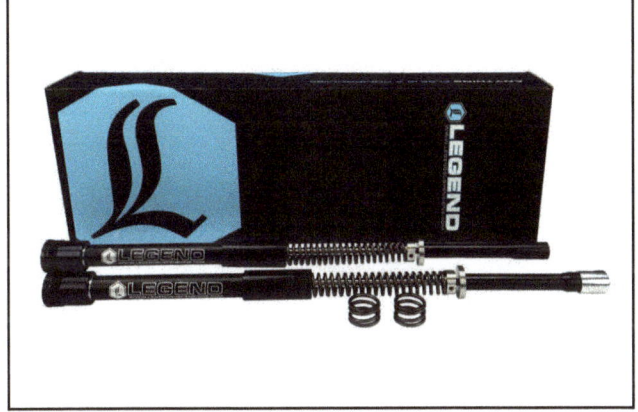

Cartridges like these allow the owner to adjust spring for weight, and damping – they come for new and older Baggers. Some have an opportunity to install an air-pressure. Some are designed for 21 and 23 wheels.

High quality shocks with spring and rebound adjustments are done by hand. Adjustable in 12 or 13 inch length, and colors of black or gold. Perfect for touring.

Top tree designed for '15 and up, Road Glide. Complete tree-kits are available as stock or no-so-stock – as well as drop trees, or 7&7 trees, some are chrome. Ness

True-Track

This True-Track shown is designed for 2009 and later.

Way back in the mid-80s I bought a new Bagger. I'd heard about the Harley-Hula for some time. And when I started riding the new Bagger with the hopped-up motor, there it was, the wobble - especially on the big sweeping curves. To me it felt like the bike had a hinge in the middle. The more I accelerated, the more the back end went back and forth until the wobble got down-right scary.

It was the famous bike builder Donnie Smith who turned me onto Will Phillips – the man who invented the True-Track. As Donnie explained it, "Will is an engineer, he works for some of the Grand Prix teams, helping them with their suspension issues. And because he's a biker, he'd experienced the hula dance, and he designed a kit that eliminated the fault. You have to buy one of his kits."

Working on the advice of Donnie Smith and other experienced builders and mechanics, I put a True-Track kit on my Bagger. And the hula was gone. I wouldn't own one of the pre-2009 Baggers without a True-Track kit. Period. For roughly $400 you get a bike that's more fun to ride and more stable at almost any speed or road.

In 2009 Harley redesigned the frame. Instead of three rubber mounts for the motor, there are four and two links. Also, the frame itself is made from heavier tubing.

To decide if you need a stabilizer with a newer frame, I asked a rider who pushes the late model Baggers hard – Paul Shadley from Shadley Bros. "Yes, they do need help, the bike has a hinge in high speed cornering. The stock shocks are poor, the bikes need better shocks. We like Legend Revo shocks with the remote reservoir, pricey, but they do the trick. And they need some type of stabilizer, Alloy Art sells one that we use for touring-bike frames."

Brock's Wheels

Brock Davidson is one of those pioneers we have in the motorcycle world. A person who's brought a long list of improvements to the two-wheel world – anyone who rides should be grateful.

Brock: how about a little background? Were you on two wheels at a young age? Yes, I rode a Bonanza minibike when I was 5 and fell in love. At the age of 12 (and 78 lbs.) my crazy drag racing neighbor let me ride his modified/10 second Z900 Kawasaki around the block. I only knew one speed - WFO so off I went! I had to circle the block twice to get stopped as my feet barely touched the pegs, much less the ground. I finally used the curb to stop and was hooked on the speed, sound and excitement of drag racing since that moment. We even installed wheelie bars on my 1978 XR-75 Honda.

When did you start the business? And was there a point where the business took off?
I built my first street/drag engine for a paying customer in 1984, but I knew I needed a "real job", so I enrolled in a local technical college's robotics program. I worked as a mechanical design engineer in the automotive special machine industry for about 15 years while running my engine/bike building service - concurrently

The BST Torque model, but don't try to buy the blue model – these are one-offs painted by Perewitz.

out of my home garage until I left my full-time job to pursue the motorcycle world as a professional motorcycle drag racer in 1999. I realized quickly that there was no money in racing – only money as a result of racing accomplishments. So, I officially incorporated Brock Davidson Enterprises, Inc in Jan 2002. The business grew at an amazing rate initially as I had gained credibility in the motorcycle drag racing world - becoming the builder/pilot of the world's first 7 second street legal motorcycle in May of 2000.

What were some of your first successful products and services? One was a simple service where I welded a two-piece "slipper clutch" together to eliminate the issues it created when launching Suzuki's newly released '99 Hayabusa from a dead stop. The second was a nitrous distribution block I developed for my race bikes, coined the "Showerhead."

The blocks worked so well that I received a call from Mike Watt, the owner of Nitrous Express, asking if I could make them at a price that would allow them to make profit selling to their dealers. That was my first experience with dealer margins also. Their first order was for 100 sets, then 200, 500, 1000?!

When did you decide to begin making go-fast components for Harley-Davidsons, Baggers in particular? Honestly, I was a diehard import motorcycle drag racer who never had any interest in Harley's at all. Through the years though, our customers got older and traded in their sportbikes for Baggers - mainly for increased comfort.

So, I decided to simply purchase one and see for myself. In June of 2013, I purchased a Road Glide Custom from my local dealership and was amazed at A: How much I enjoyed simply cruising, as it was far more relaxing than what I was used to, and B: just how terrible the bike was, mechanically, compared to what I was used to. The latter

BST wheels on the Trask Assault machines – this one is a TEK from Brock's.

helped me fit V twin product development into our mission statement.

In the past, "performance" to me meant "twist gas, yank arms out of sockets and accelerate at light speed until you see god." After the very first ride on my Bagger, I realized that "performance" could also mean taking a bike that is exceptionally heavy, doesn't stop well, doesn't turn well, doesn't accelerate quickly and rides like pooh. I started making suspension changes almost immediately and joined my friend Skeeter Todd in Sturgis of that year. The rest is history as they say. My Road Glide now has more miles on it than all of my sportbikes combined and I now own close to a dozen Harleys.

My initial goal was to have American V Twin products make up 10% of our product sales in five years. In June of 2018, they actually made up 15% of our sales and today they make up around 35% of our yearly revenue. This year we shipped to over 100 countires.

Can you point out to the readers, some of the Performance Harley parts that they might not know about? For certain the single most dramatic difference you can make to an H-D, especially a Bagger, is the addition of Carbon Fiber wheels. As a general rule; each 1 lb. that is removed from the rotating mass of the wheels is the equivalent of

A rear wheel Torque TEK, the hub on the other side is designed so H-D cushions can be used.

removing 5-7 lbs. from the static weight of the bike. When I swapped my OEM Road Glide wheels and tires to BST Carbon Fiber wheels and more Sport oriented Z-rated tires, The combined rotational weight savings was right at 30 lbs. Using our rule, the question would be, "does the bike feel 150+ lbs. lighter once it starts moving?" My answer is always the same… 'NO the bike feels 200+ lbs. lighter!" The stock brakes went from "terrible" to "not too bad" since the previous effort required to stop those heavy-ass wheels now get to stop the bike/rider combination.

The bike turns in and out with far less rider effort and rides much smoother - since carbon fiber dampens the road noise transferred to the rider instead of transmitting it through the chassis and up to the rider like metal wheels do. We also manufacture heavy duty aluminum swingarms that decrease the unsprung weight of the rear suspension by as much as 50% as well as offering Bitubo race suspension for road applications, and Brembo braking components.

Are there new products that just came on the market or will come out in the future? We have several new products in testing phases now, watch BrocksPerformance.com for additional product releases soon.

The owner of this Bagger has lost only one drag race among many. He learned that there's more to wining than just a kick-as motor – light wheels are a big part of the game.

Ohlins

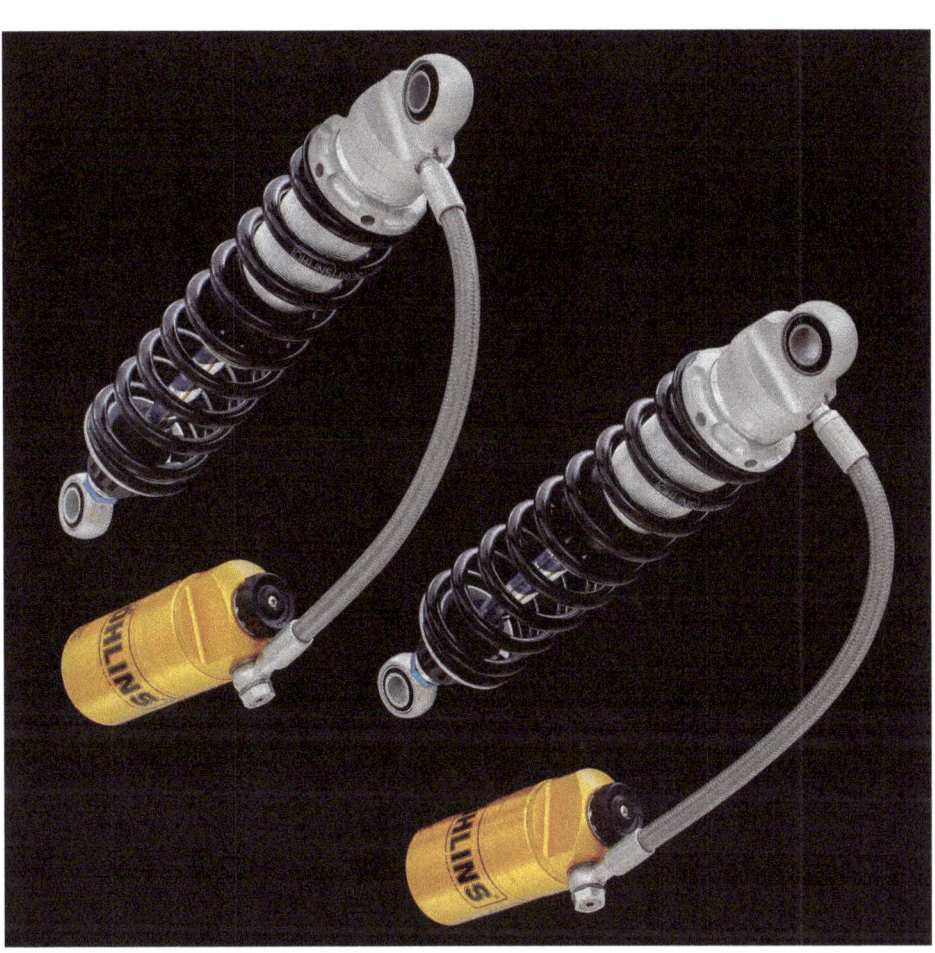

HD 357 is our fully adjustable premium choice for top-shelf performance and adjustability. Designed for the FLH / FLT Bagger chassis, the HD 357 consists of a pair of STX36 hose-mounted-reservoir shocks featuring compression, rebound, length, and spring preload for endless tuneability. Ideal for riders looking for better performance in all aspects, traction, comfort and rider feel. The HD 357 is the perfect solution for mainly 2-up riding or heavy payloads.

Joey Subrizi

What made you develop a line of high-end suspension components for Harley Baggers? We started tackling the Harley market I would say 12 years ago. The high-performance Bagger thing really started blowing up, and we started seeing it, about five, six years ago. Obviously, our background is racing, we're used in everything from MotoGP to World Superbike to Formula 1 to World Rally. Hell, we even have a NASCAR contract. With performance baggers, we could blend our experience and product line and create products that really helps the riders in that segment of motorcycling.

Especially with the King of the Bagger races that Moto America came up with, it's just over the top. Our engineers, they know how to make a motorcycle work basically because of all the history and heritage that we have from road racing. And we incorporate that technology and ideas for street bikes. We create products for these bikes that were originally meant for touring. But, you know, we've developed products to make them really go fast. And our product offers the riders comfort, control, and handling.

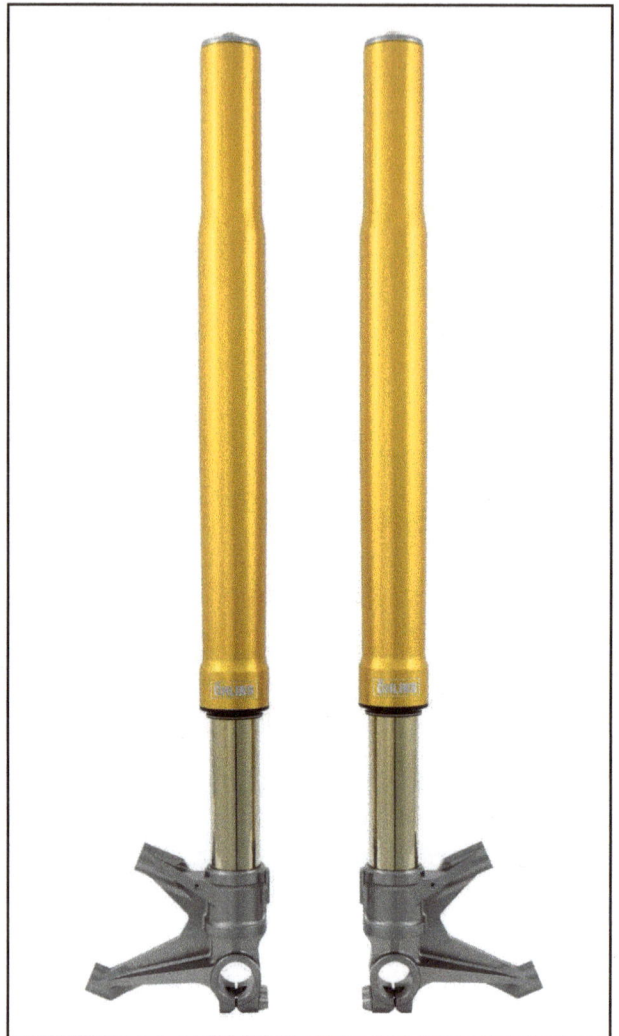

Inverted, complete fork legs from Ohlins are available, in various lengths and for various models and years.

Cool, let's talk about the forks.
Well, we have mainly two options: OK you want to improve the front end. What we do is what's known as a cartridge kit, we use the stock upper and lower tubes, but we take out all of the OEM internals and we replace those internals with our internals, essentially turning the stock fork into a set of Öhlins forks. Our cartridge kits basically will give you full rebound, full compression, and preload, all three are adjustable, making your stock fork into a fully adjustable front fork.

The next step-up is an inverted fork assembly. Some of our dealers, like Big Bear Choppers and Kraus Motor, have taken our road racing forks, an upside-down fork, and offered kits to the public. These basically let you replace your upper and lower triple trees, and the fork itself, with new brake caliper mounts. You would take your full stock front end off and replace it with a full inverted fork setup.

The new, complete, inverted fork has all the adjustments: rebound, compression, and preload. What is the advantages of an upside-down fork? The trees clamp on the smaller part of the fork - and the lower part is the bigger one. With upside-down fork, we take the bigger diameter of the tubes and clamp them into in the trees, and the smaller diameter is what goes in and out. So, you have way less flex with an upside-down fork versus a conventional fork.

The S36s are the most popular among all the shocks models. These can be ordered with different springs, and with hose versions. The length can be adjusted, also the damping adjustment adjustments.

How about the rear end. Let's talk about shock absorbers. Tell me about the shocks, and why do some have a hose going to a reservoir? Well, let me back up. We offer more than just the reservoir shocks, we offer basically three levels of shocks for the Baggers. The first one is just a base emulsion shock. That's just simply nitrogen over oil. Your only adjustability is going to be preload. Those are our entry-level models, they go for $650.

Our most popular models are the HD 159, which is a divided piston shock, meaning there's a separating piston in the head of the shock that separates the nitrogen from the oil. And they have rebound and preload adjustability. Now, our best shocks in the performance bagger market is our HD 044, which is an externally hose-mounted reservoir shock. Now we have the separating piston in the head of the shock, right? And as that separating piston is separating the nitrogen from the oil, the main piston will only have so much stroke before it'll hit that separating piston. Imagine we take that separating piston out of the shock, now you've got this whole new dimension. Now the piston has way more stroke.

Also, since we have an external reservoir, if we put a check valve in between that reservoir, that'll allow us to give external compression adjustments. So basically, when you purchase the hose-mounted reservoir shocks, you get a fully adjustable shock. You get rebound, compression, preload, and length adjustability.

So, the rider with the new very sophisticated suspension - maybe they installed the parts themselves, or dealers did. It's fair to say that most of those riders don't know how to correctly adjust the components – can you help them get the bike set up and explain how to take full advantage of the fork and shocks? Yes, a lot of times we offer setups at events like this one in the vendor area at the Harley dealership during Sturgis. Maybe the rider got the fork or the shocks from Big Bear or Kraus. It doesn't matter, we don't know if they're set up exactly correctly.

So anyway. Well, that's great, that's good for you guys. Are there other suspension mistakes? The type of mistakes I see generally is setup – that has a lot to do with everything. Setup basically controls the hydraulics and the

The NIX -22 from Ohlins is designed with all their features, and comes in a longer length.

A long-time part of the Ohlins' team, Joey never leaves home without his trusty partner.

geometry of the motorcycle.

If you get the wrong spring on the bike for your weight that can lead to a very jarring ride. Sometimes people will see knobs and they don't know what the heck they're doing, they just start turning things. If somebody completely closes off the rebound adjuster, and you go for a ride, it's gonna be stiff as a brick.

With any of these errors the bike is not going to give you that positive feeling when you go riding. And that's what we love to offer out here to our customers, making sure that the bikes are set up correctly, so the rider is happy. What if somebody buys a set of shocks and rides them for two or three years and the rider's weight changes or he carry more items, can you help" Sure, we'll put them on the hoist, get it taken care of and show 'em the changes that we made. We do give a lifetime.

We started in 1976, Kenth Öhlin, started a company basically because he was racing motocross. And he was like, «I can make something way better.» And he did, and within one year of starting his business, his team had a world championship in the GP motocross.

Chapter 4

Fairings & Fenders

What is Carbon Fiber?

Carbon Fiber is about as light and strong as anything that we see in the aftermarket "sheet metal," including fenders, bags, side-covers, and of course fairings. Seems too simple, but Carbon Fiber is made of Carbon atoms strung together in long chains, and the chains are weaved together. Resin of Epoxy is often used to hold the weave together. Different weaves are often used, think of your sweaters (or fiberglass). Companies like 3M offer sheets in different weaves and sizes. You can even buy sheets with an adhesive backing, so you can create your own small Carbon Fiber parts by carefully covering yours.

There aren't many products that have the strength and light weight that Carbon Fiber has - and that can also be shaped with standard tooling

Amazing what you can do with paint, a hugger front fender, sexy rotors and calipers, and tall bars. Klock Werks

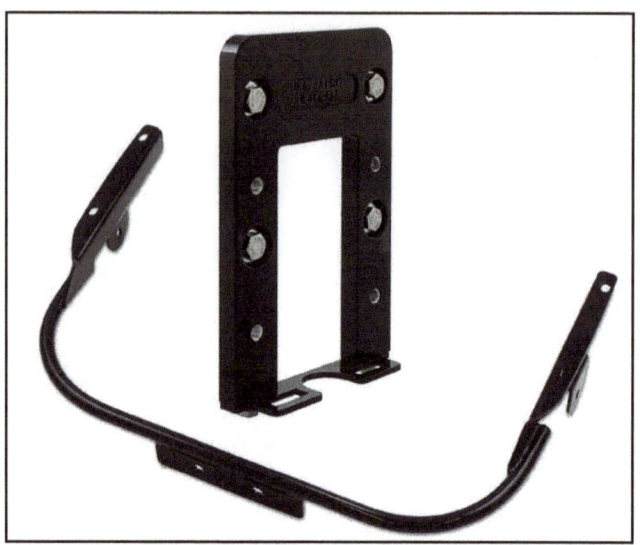

Some Road Glides look sleeker than others, and the reason may because the fairing is sitting lower and closer to the tank – done with Yaffe's kit.

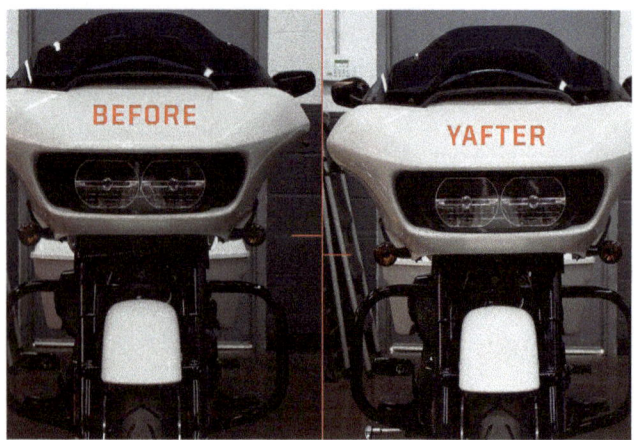

Demo photo proofing exactly how much lower one fairing is lower than the other.

like vacuum bagger or wet-up layout. Carbon Fiber is resilient to many chemicals, but gasoline is not one of those liquids – meaning that Carbon Fiber can be shaped and used for almost all the sheet metal parts for bikes or cars. Everything except a gas tank. Best you can do is buy one of the shells, available in two pieces, so the tank can match the rest of the bike. Your painter can glue them to the tank and hide the seam.

How to pick the brand of Carbon Fiber components. There are only a few companies that manufacture large items like bags, lids, fairings and fenders. There are more small items like dashes and spoilers largely because those items are easier to manufacture.

A good way to find the best true Carbon Fibers items is to check the items thoroughly. Is the surface smooth without any bubbles or runs. Whether you plan to paint your bike in your favorite color, or plan to leave the weave visible – you want a perfect surface. Inspect the edges, are they clean and smooth as they should be? Some manufacturers send fasteners with the fenders… a nice touch.

A good way to find out which brands are the best is by checking around at an event or show. Ask the riders who already have their Carbon Fiber parts - are they happy? Was it easy to paint, were they easy to install? Are there any cracks after riding twenty thousand miles? Remember that Harleys do shake. Buy from a company that's familiar with Harleys. A manufacturing company with staff and owner that ride those Harleys.

*Left:
Less is more, steel Café' front fender for Road Glides. Yaffe*

When is bigger too big

Customizing your Bagger isn't part of this book, but numerous owners are putting 21 and (sometimes) 23 inch tires on the front of their late Bagger. The shops that install the bigger wheels have some suggests - it's not quite as simple as it seems:

You can put a 21 inch on a stock Harley Bagger without a change on the bike's rake and trail (not bigger than 120). In terms of fenders, you can reuse the stock fender, but you DO HAVE to hog-out the mounting holes. Then tip the fender forward (with loose mounting bolts) then tighten the mounting bolts. Once tight, be sure to re-use the bend-tips to lock the fender bolts. Shops that do a lot of bigger front wheel installs report that, "nothing more than a 120, and even some of the 120s will rub the fender. The only answer in those situations is to use the fender extension brackets."

When you install any wheel, tire or fender, remember that the diameter of a tire expands with speed, so what doesn't rub

Above:
Lu Ventunu front fender.
Klock Werks

Right:
From Brian Klock the Tire Hugger front fender, fits 2015 to now for Touring bikes.

41

Yes, Brian's windshields come in more and more shapes and colors – this is a Kolor Flare Windshield (available in many colors), fits 2015 to current Road Glides.

An early Twin Cam Bagger with a Wrapper Gold fender (and a Café fairing). Klock Werks

in the shop might well burn off the paint on the fender at 60 or 80 mph, or worse.

A 23 inch front tire is a different animal. You can't just slide a 23 inch front wheel between the fork legs and buy a new fender. Several well-known shops have kits, they can offer the best way to get that 23 on the front of your Bagger. The good kits and shops will give you more than a cool Bagger – one that also gives you a bike that rides and handles as well before, or better before it did originally. One of those kits is from Paul Yaffe (Bagger Nation). Paul includes a 20X5.5 inch tire and a Shinko 180/55 tire. Included are the triple trees, extensions to the fork legs, extensions for the fork legs, and the extension to the neck. In the end with Paul's kit, the bike as more rake and (the important thing) the bike will have the same trail as the stock Bagger.

There are two ways to create a Carbon Fiber gas tank: bond patches of Carbon Fiber to the tank and make it part of the paint job as Brian Gall did…

… or, buy two tank-halves from Curtis and glue them to the tank - and you have a Carbon Fiber gas tank!

Chapter 5
The Drivetrain

As seen by Bert Baker

Most of the late model M-8 Baggers come with a 114 or 117 inch V-Twin. With just good aftermarket exhaust, air filter, and a tune on the dyno, it's easy to bump the horsepower to 130 or 140 horses. Add big jugs, ported heads, and a camshaft; the output will easily surpass 150 horses. Next step might be a stroker crank, and we're looking at 200 horses ready to bust out of the barn.

The stock M-8 Harley Baggers do fine with the stock drivetrain. From the clutch to the tranny to the belt, all work pretty well. For those riders, however, who just aren't satisfied with stock Harleys, heavy-duty components are often required. The goal here is to help riders of Performance Baggers determine, how many (and which ones) heavy-duty components are a good decision.

And we haven't forgotten the Twin Cam bikes. Though they start with a milder motor when new, there are a surprising number of riders with a 124 cubic inch crate motors. The catalogs are filled with various hop up kits, as well as the crate motors, and like the M-8 owners, those riders need to consider reinforcing the drivetrain.

What follows is a Q&A with Bert Baker, of Baker Drivetrain fame. This is the guy who gave riders a sixth gear before the factory did. In the mid- to late '90s, when everyone needed a 250 or 300 rear tire, Bert gave them a transmission with the drive on the right side of the bike – much better than the wider and wider spacer kits necessary to help the belt or chain clear the fat tire on the left side. He also sponsors, and participates, in the

Bert Baker is the real deal, a man who knows what works and what doesn't - because he and the crew test their driveline components on the race track.

"Run what you Brung." drag racing events during Sturgis as well as other events.

Let's start with the primary?
Yeah, the primary drive. You know, the primary drive is the standard 428 double road chain. And it works well. Harley had some troubles in 2007, the whole architecture changed. They went from a traditional 25 compensator sprocket and 36 on the basket to a, 34 on the motor and then the 46 on the clutch basket. Their goal was to slam the whole, primary, inward. And that work to achieve their goal, they had to completely redesign the compensator sprocket. And that's where they had a number of problems. All the problems related to the compensator sprocket - the lubrication – partly because the lubrication is splash lubrication - not a pressure-fed system.

I would say their compensator sprocket today is pretty well done. You know, there's some people out there, where when you start talking 150 horsepower or whatever, that want to delete the compensator sprocket and go to a fixed sprocket without that compensating action. I'm not a big fan of that because - when I was an engineer in General Motors, we talked about something called torsional signature. Torsional signature is the nature of the output coming out of the motor. The torsional signature of a 90-degree V8 is very nice and smooth. I think the most perfect engine might be a V-16-60-degree - maybe. But a 45-degree V-twin is not ideal in the torsional signature department. It's rather harsh.

A compensating sprocket smooths out those power pulses, the torsional signature. So, I'm a fan of using the compensating sprocket all the way up to stupid levels of performance. I'm also not a fan of the auto-adjustable chain tensioner. Both Harley and Baker offer a manual chain tension, which allows you to set up your chain tension with just a little bit of slack.

I like that little bit of slack because the self-adjusting chain tensioner puts a load on both the left side motor case bearings and the input bearings in the transmission - especially under higher power levels - I like manual adjustment. The adjustment is the same as it's been for a long time.

The most significant thing though, when adjusting a manual chain tensioner, a lot of people forget and miss one thing - a step of the most reverence - you have to find the high spot. In other words, it's a pain in the butt, you have to take the spark plugs out, get the rear wheel off the ground, and put it in sixth gear. Then rotate the rear wheel to turn the primary drive.

And as you turn the wheel, you observe, the rise and fall of the top section of the chain, and you need to do that because, sprockets, like the ones in the primary drive on the clutch and then on the motor output, are kind of gears, but they're kind of crude gears. What you want is to find the tightest spot, and then adjust the chain.

The guts of a Grudge Box, note the fact that all the gears are straight-cut – much stronger than helican-cut gears.

Baker has kits for drivetrains – designed for a wide range of Harleys. Shown here is a comp sprocket, and primary chain adjuster, and gaskets for late model models – one of their many kits. All manufactured in the USA.

What's next, the clutch? Yes, next we talk about the clutch. Harley, for years, as all well as other motorcycle and automotive manufacturers, strive to have the lightest clutch effort possible. Well, that's kind of a contradiction, and you know that to have a clutch that has a big torque capacity, you need to have one of those gorilla lever efforts. That doesn't get it in today's, consumer market. A lot of riders are getting up in the years, the strength of the left hand isn't as strong as it used to be. So, the manufacturers strive for a lighter effort.

Well, they came out with the assistant-slip-clutch; it slips under a high load, during both acceleration, and deceleration. When you let off the gas or downshift it will slip a little to reduce the shock load coming back through the drive train to the engine. The net effect to the rider is a lighter clutch lever.

The other way to ensure that the clutch won't slip is to install a lockup clutch. AIM was the big Japanese maker that came out with one, and I think, Screaming Eagle come out with their version of a lockup clutch. A lockup clutch is also a way to increase the torque capacity of the clutch that AIM clutch that assistance, then slip clutch initially came out with a nine-plate version, but they did come out with a 10 plate version.

Keep in mind the hub bolts to the main shaft input of the transmission, the hub is always connected to the rear wheel. If you look at a power flow diagram and walk it through, the hub is connected to the rear wheel, the basket is always connected to the output from the engine via the primary chain. And then, the plates are the in-between part that handle the transition from the motor to the rear wheel, the handoff of power, I think all that makes sense. Okay, I mean, this is my world. I think about this topic all the time, and I'm of the opinion that most people don't think about that topic.

What is your opinion on the material in fiber plates and ATF for juice? You know, there's a bunch of automotive clutch makers I'm familiar with, they all have their special clutch materials designed with a high coefficient of friction and still and be durable. I don't know which one is the best.

If I can't point out one specific clutch assembly, there is one thing I can recommend - I'm a huge fan of running ATF in the primaries for a couple of reasons. Number one: ATF was developed with millions of dollars from the automotive companies for a fluid with a low viscosity.

ATF is highly developed to lubricate, but with a minimal amount of parasitic loss. It does a good job of lubricating, and it also does a good job of carrying heat away. Then they all have friction-modifiers. A lot of people love the old-fashioned Ford type, F transmission ATF oil, because it is claimed to have the most amount of friction modifiers, which effectively increase the coefficient of friction on the clutch plates. To me, the juice is more important than the material.

The wizard knows what breaks and why – and what it takes to ensure it won't happen again.

Next, we'll move down the flow of the drivetrain into the transmission. you know, in 2007, Harley well, 2006, came out with their six-speed. And with the six-speed, all the gears are helical-cut and they have very small teeth (except first gear). They did that for a very good reason, which is, noise passed-by requirements. All vehicle manufacturers selling in this country must be held to compliance of the DOT's noise requirements. I don't know the exact details of the test, but the thing needs to be quiet.

That's what forces the 80 DB exhaust pipes and the helical gears. A spur gear - a straight cut gear - is just too noisy to satisfy the DOT requirements. So, the good thing about helical gears is the fact that they are quiet. The bad things is that they consume horsepower, they eat horsepower. Also, they have an axial component, you have two gears in motion that are contacting each other, and a helical set will have an axial component is giving up heat and friction and all the bad stuff.

A straight-cut gear has no axial component or close to zero. And so in the racing world and the performance world of Harley Davidson straight cut gears are very much more desirable and stronger with the large teeth. And that's what our Grudge Box is all about, they're all straight-cut sets. What happens to the stock transmission as the horsepower increases to 120, 130, 150 horsepower, and keep in mind it's really torque that destroys drivetrain components, it's not horsepower (though on Harley motors, the torque kind of goes hand-in-hand with horsepower).

So it's torque that destroys the third gear in the stock transmission. It's a known problem. The third-gear failure is by product of the smaller teeth on the gear pair, third gear in particular. Under hard acceleration, there's something called spreading forces, and the two shafts input and output walk away from each other. When those two shafts effectively walk away from each other, they reduce the amount of contact-ratio on the gear pair. When the contact-ratio goes down, then you have a problem.

If you want to really test your driveline components – just install a blower on one of the company's race-bike and take it to the track.

So after the clutch and the transmission, the next ... That is whether you're running a belt drive to the rear wheel or a 530 chain. People ask me when they should consider going to a chain drive – and think about a chain at about 130 or 140 foot-pounds. It also depends on a lot because a belt is a nice arrangement. It's not dirty, you know, it's they're pretty nice these days, and they're pretty strong. But, at about 130, 140-foot pounds you need to consider going to a 530 O-ring chain. 530 O-ring chains are highly developed.

If you look at the tensile strength of an O-ring chain in the particularly, you know, RK or EK, those chains, the tensile strength is over 10,000 pounds. And it's really, really, a durable solution to any problems that could come from a belt drive. They're noisier, however, so you'll never see one on a Harley Davidson these days, because they have to comply with the DOT noise rules.

Again, like the fact that a chain has a little bit of slack in it, depending on how you adjust them. And so it keeps the loads, the loads off the transmission output and then the rear wheel. I like the chain to have a little slack, whereas the belt, to make the belts be durable, you need to make those suckers, banjo-tight that's what they need to do.

Anything to add regarding the drivetrain?
Yes, the push-drive in the hub of the rear wheel. The rubber between the hub and the wheel itself does a lot to help and preserve all the other components, like the clutch capacity and lessens the shock going into the transmission. I'm not a big fan of putting different wheels on custom wheels that do not have that feature. The push drive feature, is very, very important.

Chapter 6
Crate Motors

For those who want a jump in power, without tearing the motor apart and then reassembling it (or paying someone else to do the hands-on work), there is a simpler way to get that extra power without buying a new motorcycle. Just buy a complete motor, and either install the motor yourself or have a shop do the installation.

If you're a good mechanic, then building-up the motor in your shop sounds like a good idea. Building your own motor means you get exactly what you want, no compromises. It's also likely you will save some money. However, you have to consider the down-side - it's going to take time to do all the work, including the time to have things done that you can't do. Things like boring and fitting the cylinders to the new pistons, and taking the crankshaft to the specialty shop to ensure your bottom end will stand up to some full-throttle launches.

If you've never built a Harley motor, or you want the bike back on the road in a relatively short period of time, a new crate motor may be the

There is only one company that offers M-8 crate motors and that's Harley-Davidson. They come with a warranty, they don't challenge the bike's warranty, and the latest Crate Motor is 135 cubic Inches with 143 pound of torque.

answer. It's pretty simple. You buy the motor, and those extra parts that didn't come with the motor.

If you've picked a shop to do the install, then they will likely suggest things like a certain new exhaust or throttle body, to make that new motor can run as strong as it can. Complete motors usually do not come with fuel source and ignition. Depending on the motor you buy, you may have to buy injectors and/or a new throttle body. Likewise, the finished installation isn't finished until the bike goes on the dyno.

The other nice thing about a crate motor from a company with a good product is the fact that you know exactly what you're getting, and your new motor comes with a warranty. Below are five companies with good reputations and a variety of motors. There are more companies with more options, but the five here are a good start if you're looking at getting more power with a minimum in confusion and time.

JIMS has a catalog stuffed with aftermarket parts – among those thousands' parts are the three complete racing motors made in the USA. The 120 is the smallest; the other two are 131 and 135 cubes. The 120 puts out 125 horses and 121 torque. All are Twin Cam designs and can be purchased from H-D dealers.

What is Available

Harley-Davidson

The 131 M-8 crate from H-D (now a 135-inch motor) is a good example of a crate motor. First, there's information on the H-D web site and the catalog. If you want more information (and without bias), you can look up the videos on YouTube.

The new 135 inch V-Twin puts out 143 ft. lbs. of torque, and horses that aren't posted. 4.31 inches is the bore spec for both the 131, and 135-inch motors. To find the extra four inches of displacement, H-D installed a crank assembly with the stroke of 4-5/8 inch stroke. The new motor comes with a 68mm intake manifold and injectors that squirt 6.2 grams per second. The H-D crate motor is EPA compliant in 49 states.

Additional details include a two-year warranty, when the motor is installed by a dealer within two months of the purchase of the bike. If you want to buy one of the 135 motors and your bike is more than two months old, the dealer will give you a separate warranty on the motor, the separate bike's warranty stays intact. The M-8 is available for 2021 and later bikes, the motor is not available for three-wheel bikes.

Twin Cams

The Twin Cam motors are a totally different situation. There are a number of companies that manufacture complete Twin Cam motors, not the case with M-8s.

S&S Cycle

https://www.sscycle.com/

The best-known company to produce complete motors is S&S, the Wisconsin based company that makes everything from carburetors to exhausts, the list has no end. Most of the S&S crate motors come with a two-year warranty. You can buy a S&S motor from well-known retailers, or you can buy a motor direct (though you can't just drive there and pick it up). Just start with a phone call to S&S Cycle. Visually, most of the Twin Cam motors come in silver case, chrome covers, black case chrome covers and black case, gloss black covers (Black Edition). The displacements of crate "Bagger" motors start at 111 cubic inches, then there's the popular 124, and best of best is the 143 monsters. Some meet EPA and some don't. The tune – cams, compression, and heads – differ from one displacement to another. The good example is the baddest 143 Twin Cam, they put the oil pump pickup in the back of the pan so there's plenty of oil pressure during a wheelie or a hard launch. The S&S Cycle web site has a wealth of information for each motor, and photos of course.

When you're looking for a complete motor, remember the crankshaft is part of the foundation of a good motor. Darkhorse starts by using high quality material, careful assembly, including welding, and dynamic balancing.

The factory Twin Cam bikes came (later) as 103 and 110. S&S did go just a little bit farther – with a complete 143 cubic inch motor.

R&R Cycles

http://www.rrcycles.com/

R&R Cycle makes almost everything necessary to build their motors - like the complete crankshaft, cases, cylinders, and cylinder heads. One of the advantages of dealing with a smaller company is the ability to buy direct from the manufacturer. R&R has an option list as long as your arm.

The 124-inch motor is a good example, the motor starts with a new case (with an MSO), with Timken bearings, a new R&R forged crank that's been plugged, welded and dynamically balanced with H-beam rods. Pistons are forged, the oil pump is a 3-stage design carved in house from a billet of aluminum. Likewise, the support plate is cut from aluminum in-house. Cams are gear-drive, lifters are new of course. Topping the whole thing are the stage-5 cast cylinder heads with raised-ports. The option list includes R&R billet rocker covers, roller rocker arms with different ratios, and cams of course,

124 isn't the only displacement available in the complete Twin Cams. The motors start at 103, and goes to 103, 117, 120, and the 124. You can pick the displacement, and whether it is tuned to horsepower or torque.

Ultima

http://www.midwestmcdealerexpress.com/storefrontCommerce/

Ultima manufactures' Twin Cam motors are designed to drop right in. These motors come in three displacements: 100, 113 and 124. Each one comes with Ultima's own crankshaft assembly supported on the left side by Timken bearings. H-beam connecting rods and forged aluminum pistons. Camshafts come from Andrews, and the chain is controlled by a hydraulic tensioner. Warranties differ from one motor to the next: 100 comes with a two-year warranty, 113 is one year, and the 124 motor comes with a six-month warranty.

Ultima motors (and all their other parts for that matter) can be purchased through Midwest Motorcycle Supply. You likely will see their ads in the magazines and the web sites. The Ultra site

R&R isn't the biggest shop, but this father/son team ensures quality by manufacturing almost all the components in the house. The crankshaft is all R&R parts, then assembled to tight specs for both runout and bal

The bully on the block is the 135 from JIMS. Like the others, this machine is assembled in the US from US parts – the 135 comes with a hi-volume Oil Pump. Output is 136 and 135 in horsepower and torque.

The finish on a complete S&S depends on the motor. Some are raw aluminum with limited chrome parts. Some, like this one, come with gloss black on the rocker boxes, cam cover, and pushrod tubes.

This 143 from S&S is designed to perk-up the performance for any 1999 to 2006 big twin with the exception of the 2006 Dyna.

offers a link to contact Midwest Motorcycle Supply:

Note: Ultra motors do not come with a certification from the EPA.

JIMSUSA

https://www.jimsusa.com/

JIMS is best known for the high-quality specialty tools that make working on Harleys easier and safer. Obviously, from that start making tools, JIMS has expended to a thorough, fat, catalog of aftermarket parts and assemblies for Harley-Davidsons. Among those hundreds of parts are a group of complete Twin Cams, (minus the intake and ignition), that come in displacements that include a 135-inch race engine, a close member of the family is a 131-race engine followed by a 120 inch race motor. If you're looking for a transmission that can handle the extra torque, JIMS has a variety of transmissions: 5 speeds, 6 speeds, right-side drives, and the Fat 6 – more information is just one click away.

Chapter 7

Ward Performance

Rick Ward

Sometimes called Mr. Porting. Or, Mr. M-8 heads. Whatever Rick has, he's well known throughout the industry for building motors and making cylinder heads flow. Read the Q&A below and you realize he knows way more than just porting heads.

You went to trade school after high school, and started work as a mechanic after trade school? Yes, I went to tech school for auto mechanics after high school and worked into a series of dealerships in the Minneapolis/St. Paul area. The best of the bunch was Lupient Oldsmobile because they were good about sending the technicians to the GM Training Center, so we were always on the cutting edge. The body shop manager at Lupient owned an Alcohol Funny Car, and I helped him out in the evenings and traveled nationally to the races with him.

You went from the dealerships to working for Vance & Hines, how did that come about? I became the crew chief for the funny car, and we were at the Gator Nationals in '82. I don't know what possessed me, but I walked up to Terry Vance and I said, "I want to move to California and work for you guys." It turned out to be perfect timing because a position had just opened up. They were going to start selling Pro Stock engines to help grow the class, and that was my position – building pro stock engines, dyno testing and supporting customers at the races. It was a dream job really!

How long did you work for Vance & Hines? About five years. I started in '83 and in '89 I left California to move back to Minnesota. Lori and I were planning on getting married, buying a house, and starting a family, and Minnesota seemed like the better place for that. I left on good terms. It was hard to leave, I loved my job and loved working for Terry and Byron.

Rick Ward: Started as a mechanic, managed a drag-race team, worked for Vance & Hines, opened his own shop, did more and more motorcycle motors, figured how to make a cylinder head breathe, bought a CNC, and put it all together to become one of the best porting heads in US.

So, what happened when you got back to Minnesota? I rented a little 1200 square foot building, didn't really have a good plan (laugh). I bought a work bench, jack stands, floor jack, and went back to working on cars because that's what I did before moving to California. Eventually I started working on bikes. I did a lot of work for local drag and road racing customers, and that snowballed. I worked out a deal with Byron to buy a valve and seat grinder, and a Superflow bench. I needed those pieces of equipment for cylinder-head work. By about the early '90s I was doing a lot of motorcycle heads and complete engine builds. I became busy enough that I was able to focus strictly on motorcycles.

Did you do porting and head work when you were at Vance & Hines? No, I built motors and ran the engine dyno. I didn't start doing heads until I moved back from California.

How did you learn to do all that head work? I obviously paid attention to what was working on the engines I built at Vance & Hines. I bought the Superflow, and basically taught myself from there. I read a lot of books and I tested my methods with the flow bench. It was basically just trial and error and a lot of time on the flowbench. I would grind material away and then fill back in with epoxy or clay to figure out what worked and what didn't.

By the early '90s, we figured out how to measure the cross-sectional area of a port. I bought my first computer and a flatbed scanner. We would fill the ports in the head with silicone rubber and pull a port mold. We then cut slices incrementally throughout the port, scanned the slices, and then fed the image of the scan to the computer and the computer would accurately calculate the cross-sectional area from pixels in the scan. We could then figure out where the minimal cross-sectional area was and calculate air speed. I feel we were on to that technology before most of the other shops, especially in the motorcycle industry.

There is big power to be had by taking advantage of the dynamic effects that happen during the intake cycle. Inertia supercharging is taking advantage of column inertia which is determined by cross sectional area/airspeed. The inertia of the air/fuel column will continue to fill the cylinder after the piston reaches bottom dead center.

Pressure wave tuning is adjusting overall runner length to enhance power at a certain rpm. If the pressure wave arrives back at the intake valve just as it opens for the next cycle, the momentum of the air will continue to flow into the cylinder, aiding in volumetric efficiency. By

During our busy time we have well over 200 pairs of H-D heads in the shop at any one time.

Tell us about the sequence of porting....

I'm developing a program for the Indian FTR1200 head right now. I will take you through the process…

First off, I build fixturing for the SuperFlow 1020 flowbench to attach the head using a specific bore size. I will also need a device to actuate the valves to specific valve lifts measured with a dial indicator.

We will also need radius inlets and exhaust pipe adapters to mimic the intake and exhaust systems (we will also flow test using the actual intake and exhaust).

We now have a 3D printer, allowing us to print these flow bench fixtures, which would have taken us days to machine in the past.

Once we have everything in place to flow test the stock heads, we test to get baseline numbers and see what we have to work with.

With some engines we have to work within the rules of engine displacement, Max RPM's, Valve material and so on.

We set goals for power output and RPM's. then calculate required flow, Valve and seats sizes, minimum cross-sectional area, overall intake runner length.

Usually, it makes sense to refine the stock port using the stock sized valves as a lower cost option for the street. We can usually pick up flow in the 15% range with the proper valve seat shape and CNC porting.

For an all-out race head it usually requires larger valves and seats to get to where we need to be, especially when engine displacement and RPM is increased.

Once we have met our performance goals on the flow bench. We build fixturing to locate the head on the CNC. We then measure the important locations with dial indicators and touch probes. Once we have the digitized port surfaces we import into CAD and align with our measured reference geometry.

At that point we break up the port into sections to determine how far we can come into the port with the different tools. We typically machine the harder seat area with a shorter more rigid custom 6-flute tool. The main port being aluminum allows us to use our 6" long custom 3-flute porting tool. It's a very tedious process coming up with the right tool vector point to keep the tool from shanking out inside the port, or the tool holder and spindle colliding to the head and fixture outside.

After all the individual programs are completed, I can manually edit them into one complete CNC porting program.

We are typically able to CNC port, CNC machine the combustion chamber and CNC surface the head gasket area all at once.

After the above is completed, we install manganese bronze valve guides, ream or hone to size. We then machine the valve job using our Newen Contour BB single point CNC valve seat cutting machine. We use profiles developed during the flow testing stage utilizing multiple angles and radii.

Our goal is to not have to perform any hand blending of the valve job to the CNC porting. Every now and then we come across a head that has core shift from the factory and our porting does not clean up everywhere. In that instance experience tells us whether it is best left alone or to hand blend with a porting tool. In many cases it is more cosmetics than function and hand blending does not change the results on the flow bench.

The above process can easily take 3-4 weeks to complete.

addressing both, volumetric efficiencies can be increased up to 130%.

Most of your early head work was on Metric bikes? Yes, until the mid-1990s, most of the porting and cylinder head work I did was on Metric race bikes. In the early 90's a company had manufactured a Kawasaki GPZ style, 2-valve per cylinder head that NHRA decided to allow in Pro Stock Motorcycle. We were the first to adapt that head to a Pro Stock Suzuki bottom end. It was very involved, there were many items that had to be relocated to make it work with the Suzuki bore spacing.

When did you buy your first CNC? We bought our first Mazak CNC in 1993 along with a seat of Mastercam CAD/CAM software. When I first bought the CNC, I didn't have a great plan for it, or any experience running it. I just loved the idea and the technology. I was probably like a lot of other shops thinking I would get rich off making billet motorcycle parts. I made oil pans, oiling kits, trinkets really. I spent a lot of late nights teaching myself to design and draw the parts in CAD and program the machine with CAM. It just about put me out of business, it was a very large payment due every month.

It was after I'd had the CNC for a while that I started using the machine on cylinder heads, and that changed my business forever. Cylinder head modifications became my niche, and later full simultaneous 5-axis CNC porting.

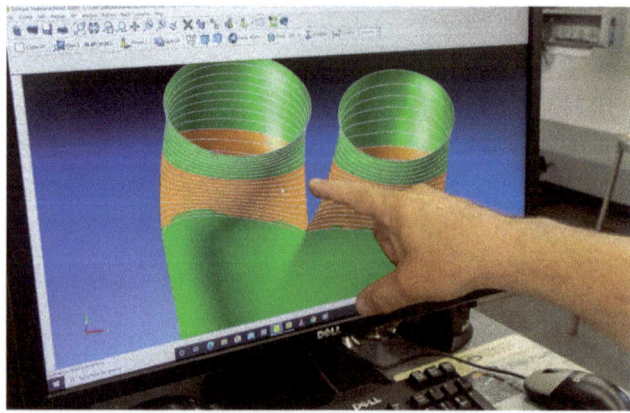

A photo of one of our H-D M-8 ports in Cad. We can measure cross-sectional area and adjust as needed. A lot of our port development is now done in CAD instead of by hand with porting tools.

How did you transition to about 100% Harley-Davidson heads? I did a set of Harley heads as a favor for a guy during the early '90s. Gradually we took in more and more porting and head work (and less engine building) and more Harley heads. When we moved in 2002, we sold the engine dyno, and discontinued engine building.

You've built all those winning motors - and learned a few essential pieces of the puzzle that makes for a really-fast motor? What are a few of those pieces?

1). With the Metric bikes they all had individual intake runners. The minimum cross-sectional area/air speed was very important. Also, overall runner length to tune the pressure wave for a specific RPM was a big deal (we spoke about this earlier in the interview). With the V-Twin, most of what I said above are non-existent - the V-Twin has a very short intake runner so there really is no column inertia. With the Y manifold pressure wave tuning is out the window. The Harley-Davidson port is really pretty ugly. It has some very sharp, beyond 90 degrees, turns, and is very hard to keep the airflow attached in the turns. When the air separates and goes turbulent it chokes off the port. For that reason, I think bigger is better - the air can stay attached at slower air speeds. Since there is really no column inertia, torque doesn't suffer by making the port larger, it is better to slow it down and keep the airflow laminar. I'm sure there are people that will argue that theory, but that's what I believe.

2). People do not choose static compression correctly. They purchase an 11:1 piston kit and think that's what they have. It may be with the correct size combustion chamber, deck height and head gasket thickness. Most don't have the tools to accurately measure cylinder head chamber volume or the piston dome/dish displacement. Also, if you had 10 people measure piston deck height you would probably get 10 different answers.

When choosing static compression ratios for the street and pump gas, I like to consider the intake valve closing timing. The piston will not build compression until the intake valve is closed. Therefore, a cam with say a 50-degree close will tolerate and actually prefer higher static compression ratio than a cam closing at 30-degrees. The higher static compression actually gets back some of the loss of low-end power caused by the longer duration/later intake closing cams.

3). Using correctly matched parts is very important. Choosing piston kits, camshafts, exhaust systems and intake systems that work for the intended use is a very big deal. We get customers that buy a piston kit from this shop, cams from another guy, exhaust because they like the look, a filter because it matches their wheels… then they're disappointed when it makes about 30 less horsepower than expected.

4). Knowing what the customer is looking for is very important. His bike, how he rides and expectations.

We have customers that want the big numbers, they want to beat their buddy, and may occasionally take their bike to the dragstrip. They just want a fast motorcycle period. This type of customer should focus their attention on the 4500 to 6500 rpm range. If this combination is shifted just shy of the rev limiter, with the rpm drop on the shifts, the engine will never go below 5000 rpm. This bike is still totally streetable - you will sacrifice the left side of the graph power to gain that performance edge. The bike will be happier when passing if you downshift a gear to put the rpms in the sweet spot 3500+ rpm. After a while it just becomes natural riding this bike - just ride it like its asking to be ridden.

Then there are people who ride two up often, might do a lot of cross-country riding. They just want it to feel strong when they roll it on at low rpm. Their usable rpm range is between 2000-5000 rpm, and their bike may never see the rev limiter. They want to just roll on the throttle to pass a car and not have to downshift. The average customer probably falls somewhere in the middle.

Any suggestions for Twin Cam and the M-8?
For the Twin Cam 103, oversized stainless

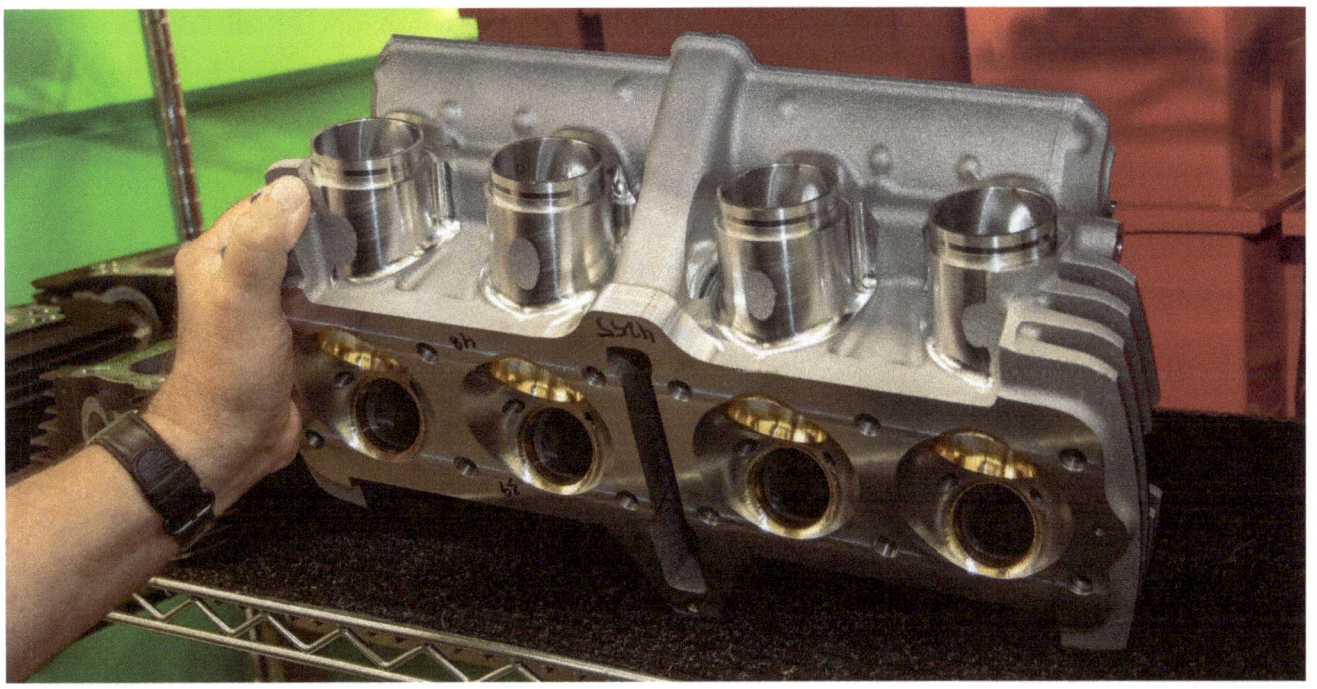

The Vortex II cylinder head is one of our most successful products. I designed it in 2000 for the Suzuki GS and Kawasaki KZ NHRA Pro Stock Bike engines. It was designed to optimize the performance of the 2-valve 1500cc engine, which had an advantage under the rules at that time. We had the head cast and did all the machining and 5-axis CNC porting in house. The head was a dominant force in NHRA Pro Stock Bike in the early 2000's. It also proved to be versatile and adaptable to other classes such as Top Fuel, Funny Bike, Pro-Mod and more. It set many records and won many titles.

valves, beehive springs, CNC porting, CNC the chambers, surface the heads so the chamber volume is compatible with the piston and camshaft combination. The customer needs to include the right intake and filter setup, along with a compatible exhaust system.

For the average 110-120 horsepower Twin Cam build there's really only one head we use and that's the stock 103 style casting from H-D with the 1.900"/1.610" valve combination.

If the customer is looking for a large displacement (124+) Twin Cam I prefer the H-D MVA/CVO casting or the S&S Superstock head. These heads have larger valves and seats, with wider valve angles, giving them more valve to valve clearance for big lift long duration cams. You will be money ahead using these heads than you would modifying the 103 casting and have a better head in the end.

As far as M-8's go we have a WP475 drop-in cam, along with our CNC ported intake manifold and a good filter setup, and good exhaust. We've seen these 114/117 cubic inch M-8's in the mid 120's for HP & TQ. That's great power and never had the heads or cylinders off. Try and do that with a Twin Cam.

There is no doubt, the M-8s have more potential because of cylinder head flow. There are still some problems, like the intake manifold - that's something that is evolving and getting more options as time goes on. As for intake ports, we can surpass 400 cfm with a +2mm-over valve. By opening the cross section at the manifold, you can add another 25 cfm to that. We have also maxed out the cross-sectional area of the stock exhaust pipe/port at about 270 cfm. With our 2-inch exhaust pipe mod, we are now well over 300 cfm on the exhaust.

The problem is the layout of the motorcycle. The intake manifold, especially for the front cylinder, is confining. Because of the placement of the throttle control on the left side of the manifold, that pushes the manifold forward, now the manifold has a terrible turn into the front head. On the flow bench with a velocity stack on the port, you get these great numbers, but in the real world the air has to get through the manifold. The currently available exhausts are limited to a 1.875" primary tube at least until you get out of the head anyway, then they can step larger.

What about even more power from an M-8?
We sell a custom 130 kit, with one of our cams, CNC ported intake and a 64mm throttle body. Along with the right exhaust, we regularly see 160+ horsepower. We were involved with the first 4.5" bore x 4.5" stroke 143 cubic inch to make over 200 hp.

I have a good customer from Michigan now making 230-240 hp and running 8 second ¼ mile times at over 150 mph with a Road King. Pretty impressive really!

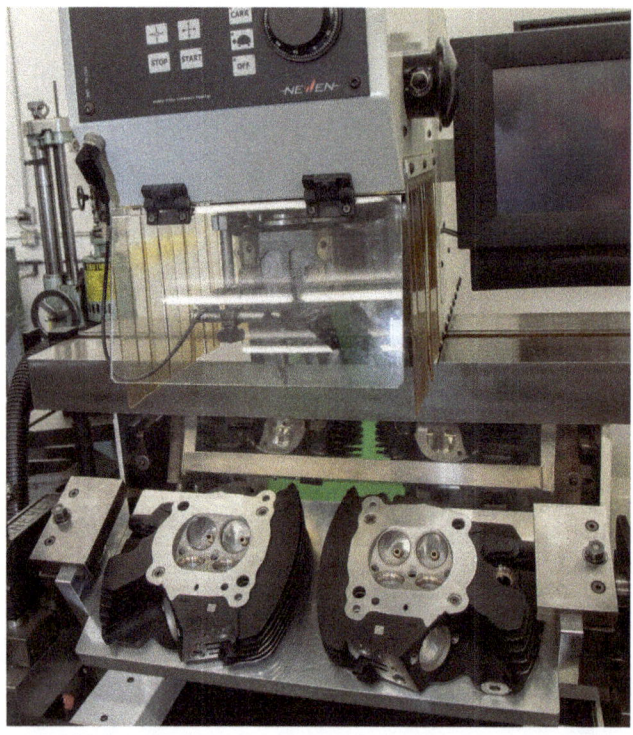

Using this machine, we can design and produce valve seats with different shapes based on computer-generated profiles that consist of various angles and radii. We can modify these profiles as needed without needing custom ground form tools. This enables faster development of custom seat shapes for improved flow. Moreover, using a single point cutter like a CNC lathe ensures perfect concentricity, unlike plunge cutting with a custom form tool. With the form tool and cutting multiple angles and radii at once, there is much deflection.

Chapter 8

Mr. Carbon Fiber

Twin Cam Bagger from Curtis

Curtis Hofman is more than just a manufacturer – he's a bike building as well. Those skills come in handy when he thinks it's time to sample their own products. The blue Street Glide is one of those projects. Though it wasn't new when Curtis pulled it into the shop, it looked like new, and the frame shared the same dimensions as the brand-new Bagger frames.

Considering the fact that this bike was to be Curtis' own ride, it had to have more – more motor. The top of the motor was pulled off, and the cylinders were replaced with cylinders and matching 10.1 to 1 pistons from Fuel Moto. While the motor was in pieces, Curtis sent the heads to Rick Ward for a porting operation, and camshafts from Woods.

The crew left the drivetrain stock; a Harley six-speed tranny and belt-drive to the rear wheel. The suspension, however, is a big step-up from stock. When you look at the front end you see Milwaukee's fork legs, but the part you can't see are the Legends AXEO21 kit. Designed

The 2015 Street Glide rolls on Pirelli rubber (21 and 18 inches) mounted on aluminum Hofmann Design wheels.
Brakes up front are Brembo calipers matched to Galfer rotors.
For suspension, Curtis picked AXEO cartridges and the Revo-A shocks, all from Legends.

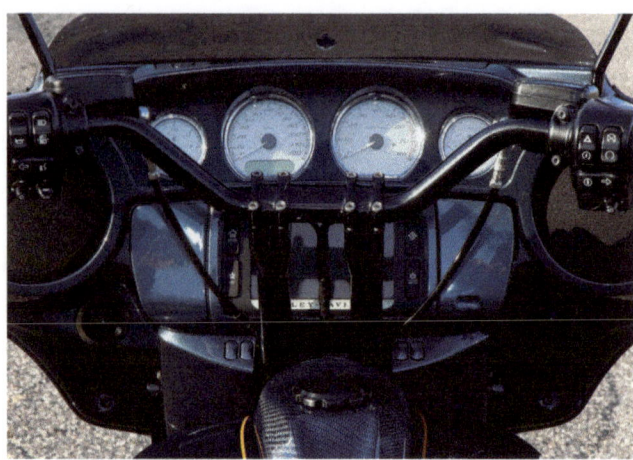

Big Bear handlebar, mounted to a riser from the same company. Controls and grips carry the H-D logo, also the gauges, mid-control Booster Brad and pegs as well.

Carbon dash from Hofmann, and a cavity on the tank for knees. Everyone wants to know what color that blue is? Curtis explained that the blue is the color of the weave, the only thing painted is the gas tank.

The bags are by Curtis, also both fenders are Hofmann's. The seat is a Drag Specialties item.

for Baggers with a 21-inch front wheel, those kits include cartridges and springs, and include pre-load adjuster for each side. The shocks in the back are from Legends as well, the REVO-A model with adjustments for rebound, and pre-load.

For brakes, Curtis installed four-piston calipers from Brembo and wave rotors from Galfer, on both front and back. The rotors are bolted to the hubs of the Hofmann Signature Series wheels, 21 inches up front and 18 in the rear. Both are wrapped with rubber from Pirelli.

Curtis does not make a Carbon Fiber Batwing fairing, but he had a long list of Hofmann parts crafted in Carbon Fiber. How about the dash, fenders, bags and side covers. When friends came through the shop and saw the components, they all said, "what color is that blue, where can I buy it?" The interesting part is the fact that the blue is not a certain paint, it's the color of the weave.

The only parts to be painted were the tank and the inner fairing. Of course, before painting the tank, the knee recesses were cut out of the tank, and sheet metal was fabricated and welded in place. Once the welding and finish is working, yes, the tank was painted to match the weave, then everything was covered with multiple layers of clear.

The controls and comfort for this Street Glide are a mix. Handlebars and the riser are both from Big Bear. On each end of the bar are grips from Harley-Davidson. The controls on the bar are from Harley-Davidson, as are the master cylinders. Mid-controls came from Booster Brad, and the pegs too. The seat with the plaited pattern came out of the Drag Specialties catalog.

When the bike was finally rolled out, Curtis had to smile. "I wanted to put all of our parts on a Street Glide," explains Curtis. "Everybody was doing Road Glides, so I'm like, let's do a Street Glide instead. I wanted the mid-controls, and the smaller fairing, no fancy stereo, not much chrome. A nice, simple machine and a good rider. Easy to ride, nimble in traffic, proud to own."

Hofmann used cylinders and pistons from Fuel Moto, heads from Ward Performance, cams from Woods and an air cleaner and exhaust from Trask to made a healthy 107 Twin Cam motor.

The primary case houses stock components – except the clutch discs. Drive to the rear wheel is the factory belt.

The Drag Bike

The red and black Street Glide is another Curtis-creation, but the project for this bike was different than any others. "We built this one for Drag and we kinda went all out," explains Curtis. "We took out all the stops. I mean it was torn down to the bare frame, then we slicked-out the frame, had it painted with candy."

"We had access to all the vendors that sell through Drag," explains Curtis. "They all said, 'Here, use these parts, these need to be incorporated.' But then we also did a lot of our own things too, our saddle bags, our lids, and our side covers. We did the gas tank a little bit different,"

For a rear fender, the crew took the old-fashioned method, explains Curtis. "The rear fender started as a RWD metal Dyna rear fender that we chopped up and modified to make it fit in the bagger frame. The front fender is a Ness product."

"We used the same, cut-and-weld process used on the rear fender, on the gas tank. Usually,

Drag Specialties asked Curtis to customize this Street Glide – to create a really nice display bike. Curtis and crew started by stripping it to the frame and sending it out for paint. The gauges are from Harley-Davidson, with handlebars from Thrashing, and risers from Trask.

creating knee recesses is just a slice on each side, filled-in with a flat piece of sheet metal that takes a right angle to meet the bulge toward the front of the tank. The fill-in on this one is longer than most, and it meets the tank bulge gradually – no ninety degree turns."

Once the tank was welded back together, all the sheet metal was sent to Brian Gall for the paint job, the painter who painted the frame. Brian likes Xotic Colurs paints, and used their gold paint as the base - before spraying the candye applee red.

While all those parts were getting painted, the crew at Curtis' shop detailed the motor with black and more black, including the covers from Ness held in place with the 12 point Diamond fasteners. Breathing is controlled by a S&S air cleaner with the traditional shape, but manufactured with Carbon Fiber. The exit route to the atmosphere is the two-into-one exhaust from Bassani.

The vendors who cooperating in this project include, MJK, with three of their four-piston calipers, mated to rotors from Performance Machine. PM also suggested Curtis run wheels from their Image Series of forged aluminum wheels, a 21 inch on the front, and an 18 inch wheel in back. The swing arm carries the Alloy Art logo, as does the fork legs. Legend shipped them a pair of pair shocks with remote gas chambers - neatly mounted between the fender and bag by Curtis and crew.

And of course, this Street Glide has to be equipped with two of Curtis' Bags. For a rear fender, the boys grabbed a steel rear fender from RWD for a Dyna, and trimmed it high so you can see more of the rear tire. Next, they cut the big knee recesses, and after a lot of messaging, welded it all together.

The mostly-stock motor is detailed with a full set of Ness covers, along with a S&S aircleaner and Bassani two-into-one exhaust.

Like everything else, the suspension parts are top shelf: like fork legs from Alloy Art, MJK four-piston calipers and rotors from PM. PM also provided their aluminum Image Series wheels, 21 and 18 inches.

The fairing was left stock. The gauge panel was painted red, the rest is black. Kickers donated the entire tune-system, include the speakers in the fairing of course.

The final assembly included more of the showcase from the catalog. Risers from Trask, bars from Thrashin' equipped with grips from PM. Floorboards and foot controls carry the initials MJK.

"All in all, the bike seems at first to be just a big showcase from the Drag catalog," explained Curtis, "but what separates the bike from a completely bolt-on bike, is the details. Like the great paint including the frame, and the fabrication necessary to create the recesses and the one-off back fender. There's creation here, and that ensures that there are no Baggers, quite like this one."

The left side provides a good view of more add-ons: like Legend's shocks with remote gas chamber, Alloy Art swingarm, chain drive conversion, and another MLK four-piston caliper. The wild and loud paint job (and frame) is the work of Brian Gall.

Q&A with Curtis

Let's start with some history? I always worked in MC shops, dealerships and aftermarket both, always worked on bikes. When I moved back from California I said screw it, I'm gonna do something on my own and do what I wanna do. Once in Minnesota I began sharing a 1200 square-foot shop in a building that was all shops, and before too long I took over the next-door bay for myself. I moved four times quickly. Each one bigger than the one before. 2021 was the fifth move.

You were one of the first builders to embrace the Performance Bagger concept. You were an early bird. What was it about Performance Baggers that you liked? We were coming off the complete opposite - we'd been building big-wheel Baggers. We did a lot of innovative things and made a name for ourselves. The shop got so busy I was always working. Sometimes I got to the point where I would grab a bike and go out for a ride. On the short rides I noticed the starting sequence: Start the bike, air up, release the fail-safe.

Curtis Hofmann is always on the move – the young man who saw an opportunity and took a big risk to manufacture Carbon Fiber fairings, bags and fenders. As time goes, there are more and more parts in Curtis' catalog.

So that's when the light popped on for me in 2015, that's when I started building Performance Baggers. I just wanted something fun that I can beat on and not have a problem. I just want to get somewhere where I can turn off the bike, walk away, and not worry about parking, not worry about dragging a saddle.

What made you start your own line of Carbon Fiber parts? With our first of the Performance Baggers, we put in big motors, big brakes and good suspension. We left the sheet metal stock. Which meant it was heavy. So, we started to think about carbon fiber.

You look at Ferraris, Lamborghinis, Maserati, and even the new Corvettes and Camaros – Carbon Fiber is part of the performance game. Basically, we found the void in the market.

It took us about a year and a half to develop everything, do the research first, and then made the tooling. We released the first parts in the spring of 2017.

I didn't want to manufacture small pieces. We released saddlebags, saddlebag lids, rear fender and side covers before we let anybody know what we were doing. A complete back-end for your Bagger. That's what we released originally, we spent a lot of money and wondered, is this going to catch on? I didn't release the front fender until December 2017, eight months after the back-end. That is still our number-one seller.

It was a big gamble to do those parts all at once. But we're OK now. I mean we pride ourselves on quality. We have brand-loyal customers, and they just keep coming back and back and they're referring us to their friends.

No, you can't call this a Performance Bagger, though it started out as a Road King and it has bags. The motor is a 124 Twin Cam, with a stock six-speed tranny, and chain drive. The frame is stretched six inches, neck is at 32 degrees, trees are from HHI, holding Legend forks legs. On the other end the swingarm from Trask is longer than stock, and supported from two Legend Revo-A shocks. All in all, Curtis started with a clean sheet of paper and this is what he built.

Part of what separated our company from others is the fact that we are a motorcycle shop. We build bikes for ourselves and customers. We try to make parts people need and are easy to install. The Carbon parts are a good example, the front fender requires only that you take out the four bolts and then install the new fender with bolts and spacers supplied with the fender. No prep and/or painting, no alignment, just four bolts and the spacers.

Isn't that a big advantage to the buyer – the fact that you design and manufacture your own parts? Yes, I think so. I think Carbon Fiber looks cool, and there's a weight savings and an increase in strength, that's an advantage. And they have to look perfect.

I'm sure you have parts that fit the M-8 Baggers, what about Twin Cam Baggers, and even earlier Baggers? Well, our parts go back to 2009, the M-8 Bagger frames are essentially the same as the 2009 Twin Cam frames. You can retro-fit fenders, bags and lids easily to early Baggers with just a little modification to the bike – not the part. You can put a 2014 and latter set of bags on a 1994 if you want. You just have to buy the hardware and the hinges when you assemble the bags. We sell a surprising number of components to the Twin Cam owners. A guy who bought one in 2012 or 2014, they love the bike. It's the same machine except for the motor.

The M-8 guys and gals, they want the best, and the Carbon sheet metal is just one part of the plan. They like the looks of the parts and the quality. A lot of them don't paint the parts, they leave the weave visible. And if they do paint the Carbon Fiber, they find that the parts need very little prep, which keeps the cost down.

In the Hofmann shop there are motorcycles, and a wide variety of Carbon Fiber parts getting ready to ship out.

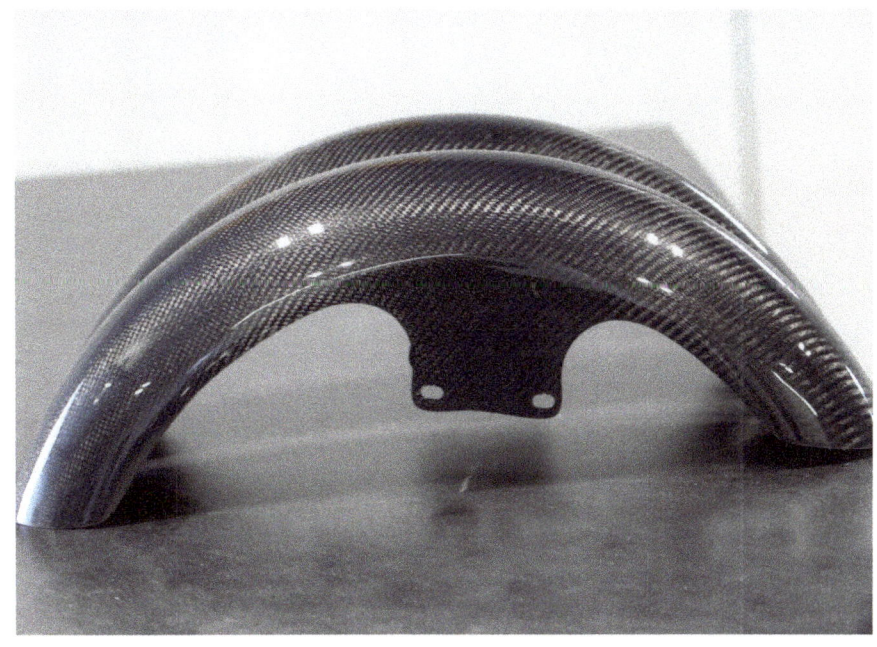

As time goes on, there are more and more fender designs, and more fenders to fit more bikes.

Chapter 9
Not John's First Bagger

John's first Bagger is the Twin Cam seen nearby. His second Bagger is a very different from the first Bagger. There is one thing, however, that's the same with the two bikes, and that is the details seen in both Harleys. Both bikes are build-up from the frame and whether if it's the fasteners, the paint, or the controls, everything is done correctly, and everything looks like it belongs on the bike.

For sheet metal, John chose mostly Carbon Fiber from Curtis Hofmann. Starting with the hugger fender up front, to the rear fender and the bags, you see the sexy weave. Side covers, and dash are more components from Hofmann.

The gas tank is a story of its own. Marshall Starrett Fabrication started the creative process by cutting a recess for John's knees in the back of the tank. Of course there are no Carbon tanks, so the next best thing was to wrap the steel in Carbon Fiber. Next, Brain Gall, from Finishline Design,

This is John's second Bagger, different but similar in the way he planned carefully and then followed through on the plan. Like the 2013 bike, the 2019 Road Glide came all the way apart, and so did the motor.

painted the tank white and bronze with big areas covered with only clear so the weave shows through.

With most Harley V-Twins, it's easy to leave the cases in the frame and install oversize cylinders. With John's, once the sheet metal was off, it seemed only logical to pull out the motor and send it to the local motor-guru by the name of Rick Ward.

Rick pulled the motor apart, including the cases, and installed a Darkhorse crankshaft, with the stock 4.5 inch stroke, and a set of Carrillo connecting rods. Next, he bored the cylinders to 4.280 inches for a total of 130 cubes. The heads of course received the CNC porting and larger-valve treatment from Rick. To complete the breathing of the new M-8, Rick installed a WP 550 cam, a 64mm Screamin' Eagle throttle body and an air filter from S&S. Getting the spent air out of the cylinder is just as important so the fresh air can get in, and for help there Rick suggested a Burns two-into-one exhaust.

When it came time to assemble the chassis, John insisted the best again. The popular Ohlins fork legs, mounted in triple trees from Krause, replaced the stock front end. In back, it's a swingarm from Trask supported by two, Ohlins' top-shelf shocks with remote gas reservoirs.

Rounding out the chassis are the four-piston calipers from Beringer – two in front and one

All the body parts seem to be Carbon Fiber, even the gas tank. The tank of course is steel, but Carbon patches were glued to the tank in the recesses and left in clear. So the whole bike is Carbon Fiber from one end to the other thanks to Brian Gall.

If the paint job was thorough, so was the motor. New jugs were bored to 4.28 inches, combined with a stock 4.50 crankshaft for a total of 130 cubic inches. Heads of course went to Ward's shop and the cam is Ward's 550. He suggested a Screamin' Eagle 64mm bore, and John picked Burns for the two-into-one exhaust.

Up front there are two, four-piston Beringer calipers and rotors from Galfer. The fork legs are from Ohlins mounted in Krause triples.

in the rear – paired with wave rotors from Galfer. The mag wheels are 19 up front and 18 in back, with Dunlop tires, 130/60/19 and 130/55/18.

The final assembly included a heavy-duty clutch, and otherwise stock components in the primary housing. The transmission is likewise stock, but looking carefully at the finished bike, you can see a multiple of non-stock components – and most of them carry the MJK logo, then became MJK, and now it's part of Krause.

In the drivetrain there's a MJK chain conversion and a hydraulic clutch cover on the right side of the tranny. Floorboards, front

Look at the gas tank, and after looking at the recess for the knees, the tank does look like a tank made of Carbon!

and rear, are colored that same MJK gold, as is the shift link. Risers from Krause hold the Fly Motto handlebars (both black) and both master assemblies are Beringer products.

When Rick Ward, Brian Gall, and the Blaine, Minnesota Harley dealer finished the assembly, it was time to fire it up, and put a few miles on the new machine before Rick Ward could put the bike on the dyno. Considering the displacement, the turnout was pretty good: Horsepower, 174 and torque, 154. John says that when accelerating in the lower gears, he has to be careful – because the back end wants to pass the front.

Above: While most Bagger builders use hand controls from Harley-Davidson, John chose controls from Beringer – known for their quality and innovative designs.

Right: Hangin' on the back are the bags that really are made of Carbon Fiber and painted so every can see the weave. The rear fender is made from the same material by the same person responsible for the Carbon Fiber bags.

Take a peek and you will see a hefty swingarm supported by Ohlins shocks with remote gas chambers, and the chain-drive conversion from MJK.

The First Bagger

Most owners of custom Harleys own more than one motorcycle. John Sandberg is no different, and his two bikes are Baggers. A more accurate description would be one Custom Bagger with a performance twist. John's crazy wild Bagger is a 2013 Twin Cam Road Glide, though it doesn't look much like a Harley Road Glide today.

When John built this Twin Cam Bagger, he didn't go halfway. Note, the stretched tank and dash, bags with integral side covers, and the speaker lids. Between the two bags is the tail-dragger fender. Air suspension allows the bike to sit right on the concrete.

The one thing people see first and last is the paint. You could call it a panel-paint job, and each panel, bordered in silver, is different than the others. The bright and complete paint job is the work of another legend from the TwinCities, T.J. Design

Because this one could be categorized as a custom Bagger – people might think the

In 2013, there weren't too many Bagger owners looking for performance, the one seen here was certainly built for looks (and performance). The point of this machine is the paint, a panel paint job done with great detail, done in TJ Design. There are a number of nice details on this bike, especially that crown, painted and screwed on to the valve stem.

performance part was left out. John, however, did not forget the go-fast part of having a cool motorcycle.

Power for this two-wheel showboat is a 124 cubic inch V-Twin from S&S, and the considerable power travels through a stock primary, a heavy duty clutch and a stock six-speed tranny. Connecting the tranny and the 18-inch mag rear wheel and Dunlop tire is a factory belt. The matching front wheel is wrapped with another Dunlop tire, 19 inches in diameter.

Above: Air suspension makes for a bike you can drop down on the ground when parked. Primary is pretty much stock, the final drive is the factory belt. Cool floorboard and curved shift lever, both are perfect parts for the shift lever and linkage.

Right: It's one of those paint jobs where the more you look the more you see! Nice the way the tank tails wrap around the custom seat.

More details: the transmission and other parts behind the motor are painted or powder coated to match the 124 from S&S – motor itself is all black except for shiny fins and the bright fasteners.

Chapter 10

The Three Baggers

Bike One

It's funny how one built-motorcycle makes the way for another and another. Sometimes, the design and features are copied the way the same. Other times a bike goes a new way and sets the stage for new designs and new looks, builders are challengers to take a risk and break out.

The case here of three bikes is a case where the first Road Glide set the path for two more.

Bob Garone is a man who owners a garage filled with motorcycles. A true motorcycle lover, there are at least 60 two wheelers in his garage and most of them carry the H-D logo. Old, new, stock, and customized, the collection gets bigger every year.

Like so many Harley-Davidson fans, Bob Garone saw the trend - all those hopped-up

This Twin Cam Bagger is about as nice and thorough as a 2016 Performance Bagger can be. Aesthetically, the Shadleys started with a new, black motorcycle and made it even blacker. The hugger-style front fender is from RWD. A subtle improvement, but a lot of people don't see, is the effect of the Yaffe bracket that lowers the fairing and moves it back slightly.

Baggers on the street and decided he needed one too. So down to the dealer he went and a 2016 Road Glide went home with him. That new Bagger didn't stay in Bob's garage for long – the next stop was the Shadley Bros shop in Whitman, Massachusetts.

Mark Shadley started the conversion from stock to one of those large Sport Baggers, by tearing apart the new motorcycle. The disassembly was thorough, including the motor. In fact, the motor was the first thing Mark tore apart. The Twin Cam came as a 103 motor, and it just happens that S&S offered a kit to convert the 103 to a 110 cubic inch screamer.

The S&S kit was suited for this project. The S&S 110 Ultimate Power Pack shipped with cylinders, 10.5:1 forged pistons, ported heads, 585 cams, adjustable pushrods, and all the necessary smaller nuts, gaskets and bolts necessary to make the kit complete.

To be sure the Twin Cam can suck in as much air as possible, Mark installed a 58mm Screamin' Eagle High Flow Induction module, paired to an air filter from Performance Machine. And to ensure there's enough gas being squirted into that air, the pair of the high flow 5.5 G/second injectors that came with the kit were instilled. For exhaust, Mark ordered a B4 two-into-one system from Bassani.

Most of the drive train was left stock, belt final drive and

The photo angle does a good job of showing the license bracket from Cycle Visions, the LED lights from Ness, and Performance Machine Floorboards.

The healthy 110 motor is thanks to Mark Shadley and the kit from S&S - complete with pistons, cams, ported throttle body and ported heads. The two-into-one exhaust-pipe is from Bassini. The end effect of all those parts and work is a dyno run that turned 115 Horsepower and 118 torque feet.

Along with the Performance Machine Floorboards is the shifter lever, the link to the transmission, and the brake lever on the other side.

stock transmission. The only real modify to the drive is the SE heavy duty spring plate.

If this big beast is going to stop on a dime and go around corners like a Ducati, it needed some chassis modifications. Up front, the factory fork legs were disassembled, and Race Tech springs were installed. Bolted to those legs are two, six-piston calipers from Performance Machine, squeezing floating, 13-inch rotors from Performance Machine. On the other end, Mark left the stock brakes in place, with the four-piston caliper and the 11.5-inch rotor.

To improve the rear suspension, the stock shocks were replaced with 13-inch shocks from Legend. Their Revo gas models, without a remote canister. Like the stock shocks, the factory wheels

The dash is a sleek piece from RWD, and of course painted black. Gauges with white faces and chrome trim look great when they're surrounded by gloss black paint.

were set aside. In their place, black, contrast-cut wheels from Performance Machine took their place. Up front the wheel measures 21 by 3.5 inches, wrapped in a 120-17 from Metzler ME 888. On the back end, it's another PM rim, 16 inches by 5 with another 888 Metzler, 180-65.

The only painting done in the Shadley booth is the front hugger fender from RWD. The bike came with the chrome package, a shame as the Shadleys blacked-out some parts. The lower legs for example, and some other bits, went to the powder-paint shop where they sprayed on the black power before puttin' before they're set in the oven.

The Twin Peaks handlebars come from LA Choppers; mirrors carry the Ness logo. Mounted to the bars are the Renthal wrap grips, and controls from Performance Machine. Closer to the ground are the pegs and floorboards, all from PM. For comfort Mark picked a Wide Tripper seat from Mustang.

Three months after the Bagger was unloaded in front of the shop, the bike was started up for the first time. After careful break-in and putting some miles on the speedo, Mark rolled it onto the dyno and the chart read out: 115 horses and 118 for torque, and Garone had himself one hot rod Bagger.

The seat is two-up and trim, with stitching by Mustang,

Outside, the lower legs are power coated. Inside, the forks are the Race Tech springs. Bolted to the legs are the sexy, PM six-piston calipers, and matching rotors.

Garone Bagger Two

Bob Garone liked that Twin Cam Road Glide. With 115 horsepower, Bob could really roll down the road, there wasn't much that he couldn't pass. All was good until 2017 when Harley-Davidson introduced that new 114 inch M-8 with four valves.

Suddenly, 115 horses wasn't enough, especially after Mark bought a M-8, and bored the cylinders from 4.016 to 4.25 inches, ported the heads, installed a lumpy camshaft and installed an oversize throttle body. Suddenly Bob was looking at Mark's taillight when they rode together.

When Mark bought that 2019 Road Glide, Bob bought one too. When Mark ordered a 4.25-inch kit from S&S with forged 10.5 forged

The Twin Cams are old stuff with the introduction of the M-8 in 2017. Thus this is the hot rod now. Front brakes are six-piston calipers from Performance Machine mated to the PM rotors. Front wheel measures 21 inches wrapped with a Dunlop American Elite tire. H-D front fork is filled with a High Performance Kit from Legends.

pistons, Bob told the boss he wanted one too. And when Mark's heads went to Rick Ward's shop, there were four heads in the package.

Me-too included most of the motor-build, including the 62mm throttle body, 550 cams and an air filter with the Trask signature. Exhausts are a front pipe from Fuel Motor Triple X combined with S&S High Roller Mufflers. The driveline was left stock, with the exception of a Barnett Scorpion Clutch.

Suspension components are made up of Legend Axeo 21 kit for the forks, while in the back a stock swingarm is supported by a pair of 13 inch Legend Revo ARC shocks with the remote gas reservoirs.

Bob's Road Glide rolls on Performance Machine wheels that measure 21 and 16 inches. The tires carry the raised Dunlop American Elite lettering and the sizes – 130-60-21 and 180-65-16. Slowing the 800-pound bullet are two, six-piston PM calipers up front, and hiding behind the saddle bags is one, stock, four-piston caliper and rotor.

The hugger front fender is from Klock Werks, and that fender is the only non-Harley body parts on the bike, it's also the only piece that had to be painted in the Shadley booth. The fairing might, however, look somehow different than

A stock tank this time, handlebars are Sport Monkey Bars by Yaffe, and mirrors from Ness. What isn't stock is the front fender, painted in the factory color.

What you can't see is the stock swingarm, the Legend shocks with remote reservoir, or the belt drive to the rear 16-inch Performance Machine wheel, wrapped with a Dunlop American Elites.

79

Inside the primary is a stock double-chain and the heavy-duty clutch. Cylinders are obviously aftermarket (from S&S) with a 4-1/4 inch bore. The crankshaft is stock (4-1/2) so this M-8 is a 128 inch motor…

most, and that's because of the fairing lowering kit that positions the faring lower and closer to the gas tank. And of course the windshield is another item from Klock Werks.

Bob picked the floorboards and controls; the boards as well as the brake, grips and shifter lever came from PM. Mirrors came from Ness and the license bracket and taillight lens from Cycle Vision. Yaffe pointed the way with his Monkey Bars.

When Bob stopped at the shop to pick up his new Bagger, he was impressed with the profile and the details. There is one more thing about this new Bagger, however, far more important than the aesthetics. The satisfaction came during the first ride with the group, running with Mark at the front. This time, Bob was running along with Mark at the front, no more looking at taillights.

… the pistons have 10.5 to 1 compression. Before the cylinder is topped off the head went to Ward Performance for a CNC porting session. Controlling those oversize valves is a 550 camshaft from WP. Feeding fuel and air to those heads is a 64m throttle body, and aiding the exhaust is a Fuel Moto Triplex front pipe, with S&S High Roller Mufflers. All those parts and skill created a hot rod motor with 146 horsepower and 149 torque.

Bike Three

Mark Shadley has likely built as many Performance Baggers as anyone in the business. When he bought the 2019 Road Glide, he thought through all the Baggers he's built in his head and picked the bikes he liked the best. His favorites. Considering the fact that Mark and bro Paul are known to ride their bikes from California to Sturgis at a pretty good clip, Mark wanted the new Bagger to be more than fast. He wanted fast and comfortable. Comfortable in the sense that after running a long day running at speed - the rider isn't worn out.

He knew the S&S "128" inch kit would net him nearly 150 horsepower – a motor that would pull and pull all the way from off-idle to the red line. Between the motor and the rear wheel, the

Even if you aren't crazy about flames, on this Bagger they did liven up that black motorcycle.

Like the number two bike, the factory legs are filled with an AERO 21 Kits. In the back the suspension is another set of Legend shocks with piggy-back reservoirs.

Left: A 128 motor - stock bottom-end mated to a pair or oversize cylinders and pistons from S&S, topped with Ward heads (and a 550 Cam) feed by a 64mm throttle body and a Trask air cleaner.

Right: Front brakes are H-D calipers, with Ness rotors bolted to a 21 inch Ness wheel, with a Dunlop American Elite tire. Front fender is stock and works fine with a 21 inch wheel.

components are surprisingly stock. Of course, the stock clutch assembly was replaced with an aftermarket heavy duty clutch. The transmission was left alone, as was the belt drive to the rear wheel.

What separates the two Glides are smaller things like handlebars from L.A. Choppers instead of Yaffe, and a seat from Drag Specialties rather than Screamin' Eagle. What is used in both bikes, (and from Yaffe) is the mounting bracket to reposition both fairings.

The biggest difference in the two bikes is the paint – what could be better than bright candy apple-red flames that fade into burnt orange laid down on a black background. The black is the work of the Shadley shop, but the art is the work of a legend by the name of John Hartnett.

Thus, the black Glide with flames, the one that set the design for Bob's Bagger, was designed for more than just a fast Bagger. What Mark created is a new category, a Touring Performance Machine.

A close-up. The flames look great especially when the paint is PPG Candy Apple red, and applied by John Hartnett.

Mark Shadley on his touring machine – like a lot of Performance Baggers this bike doesn't sit in the garage, it's on the road whenever he can get out of the shop.

Chapter 11
Big-Wheel Softail meets Performance Bagger

Performance Bagger is currently the hot phrase in the world among Harley-Davidsons. The obvious starting point is a late-model Bagger. At the top of the to-do list is to hop-up of the motor. Next comes the suspension; out goes the fork assembly, replaced with an upside-down assembly. Same applies to the rear, high quality shocks. The driveline comes in for improvement as well – it all depends on how much motor the driveline has to handle. The one thing that owners and builders of custom bikes almost always do, is apply a very nice and bright paint job. Yes, some of the Performance Baggers roll out of the shop with a complete paint job, but just as many owners don't paint their hot Bagger.

On the other side of the street there are builders like Kory Souza from Florida. Kory is a well-known builder of big-wheel Softails equipped with air suspension, ape-hanger bars, tail-dragger rear fender,

Photos by: Alex Paris

Kory Souza, king of big-wheel Softail, was challenged to make a bike that's as fast and comfortable as a Bagger.

and the essential front wheel measuring 26 inches or more. There's one more essential feature of every Kory bike - the killer paint job.

Now, only a crazy person would try to blend the two very different machines - to build what you might call a hybrid. But that's exactly what Brock from Brock's Performance, and Kory Souza, decided to do.

"Brock and I met on a ride," says Kory. "We started to talk and Brock said he really liked the way the big-wheel Softails draw a crowd. He wondered if I could build a performance bike, with his wheels and a great paint job. I explained to Brock that I would like to build him a bike. A fast bike, but I wanted to keep my look. And to do that I would have to keep the 26, the big front wheel."

"I've encouraged Performance Bagger builders to use my Carbon Fiber wheels," explains Brock, "and a number of builders did install the Carbon wheels on their project Baggers. The bikes they built are great machines, and fast, but they all look similar. Partly because most of them don't paint the bike, or if they do, they paint them in a solid color. So, I took my idea to Kory Souza, a bike builder best known for bright big-wheel Softails. I wanted

Kory started with a 2014 Softail frame, though it doesn't look like a frame from Milwaukee - the neck's been move forward, and mounted in the neck is the triple trees that push the wheel even farther out in front.

A good look at the bare frame in the shop, and a genuine Twin Cam motor with an extra 10 cubic inches to make it a 120-inches-fast . The "painting' isn't paint, it's a very durable coating often used on guns and industry.

something that would stand out from all the other bikes in a crowded parking lot."

Kory picked a 2014 Fat Boy as the foundation for the new Performance Machine. For the go-fast part of the equation, Kory bought a 110 inch Screamin' Eagle Twin Cam motor. By the time the V-Twin was ready for installation, the V-Twin was displacing 120 cubic inches and turning the same number of horses on the dyno. Before assembly, the heads, cylinders and cases were powder coated to match the frame, while covers on both sides were sent out to be coated in a light tan Cerakote treatment. To make sure the drivetrain would stand up to the Twin Cam, Kory and crew installed a set of Baker gears, a Trask Red-Basket with lock up clutch, and chain drive to the rear wheel.

To get what he calls "the look," Kory started at the front of the chassis. When all the cutting and fabrication was finished, the neck was two inches out and another two inches up. The neck itself was set at 35 degrees. The triple trees from HHI added another 9 degrees to the rake of the conventional fork tubes.

For rear suspension, Kory threw out the stock swingarm and shocks. "We designed a swingarm on the computer, two inches wider than stock," explains Kory. "The design uses two shocks

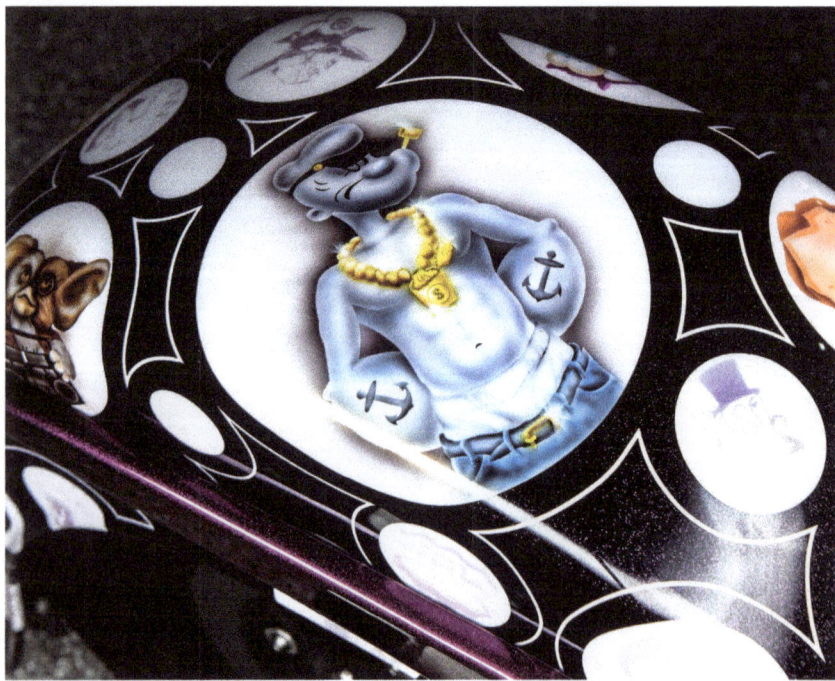

Top: The Carbon front wheel from Brock measures 26 inches, 3.5 inches wide. Mounted on the wheel is a Shinto 120/50-26. Front fender is a Kory Souza Original.

Center: The swingarm is unique - cut out of a block of aluminum by Kory, designed to use air shocks where you can see them instead the two hidden under the tranny. While he was grinding away the aluminum, Kory cut away enough material to accommodate a fat 200/50-18 on another Carbon wheel.

Bottom: If you want a crazy (and well done) paint job, Ryan Hathaway is the artist to call. No one knows where Ryan found Popeye and a long list of faces, but it doesn't matter because that paint job always draws a crowd at a show or outside a biker bar.

mounted in the more typical location with one on each side supporting the swingarm. The arm itself was cut on a CNC machine from a solid block of aluminum."

As promised, Kory used a 26-inch front wheel, a Carbon Fiber example from Brock's, 3.5 inches wide wrapped in a 120/50 tire. In back Kory took full advantage of their one-off extra-wide swingarm by mounting another of Brock's BST Torque Tek Carbon Fiber wheels, this one measuring 18X5.5 inches mated to a fat 200/50 tire.

While Kory and crew were fabricating and assembling, painter Ryan Hathaway was busy in his paint booth. First came the frame and chassis components, painted a bright magenta. The sheet metal came next. At first glance it looks like the sheet metal is painted black, decorated with too many crazy graphics to count. Look closer however, and you see the magenta flakes throughout. It is, as Kory promised, a crazy paint job.

Kory Souza has likely built and ridden as many big-wheel Softails as anyone. So, he knew exactly what to expect on the first road test. "But this bike felt way different," recalls Kory. "It's those wheels. With typical wheels, when you lean - it turns. With the Carbon Fiber wheels, the reaction is so much faster. All you have to do is look to the side, and it turns."

"I like all the bikes I build, but this one is special – with the paint job that's crazy (even for me), the wheels, the hot motor and the swingarm that we crafted – this is one to keep."

At the front, there's the Inverted fork with radial mounting for two, four-piston Brembo paired with rotors from Ness. In the middle there's another driveline component with that same tan coating and the exhaust pipe with a Stupid Fast muffler. Note the chain drive and the fender from Klock Werks with modification from Kory.

Chapter 12

Motorwitch

FXR on Steroids

Readers might wonder what a FXR is doing in a Bagger book? Well, what looks like an oversized FXR started life as a Road King Special. Once in the hands of the Motorwitch, however, the brand-new Harley was stripped to near-nude. "Harley-Davidson gave me the bike for the Born Free show," explains Danny Wilson. "When Harley offered me any bike, I knew I didn't need a touring model. I didn't need a fairing, big bags, and lots of accessories. I wanted a narrow motorcycle."

With the bike stripped, Danny put the Road King in a diet. "I found a battery that was small, but met the cranking specs for a M-8. Out came the stock battery, and a much smaller lithium, battery went into the same location." Anyone who's looked under the seat or behind the side-covers on a late-model Bagger realizes that there's a lot of bundled wire, junctions and the larger-gauge. There's a reason those side covers are bulging out.

The smaller battery left room to rearrange the harnesses and suck everything within the limits of the frame tubing. The stock side covers went in the pile of not-needed-parts, and Danny went to work fabricating the concave "FXR" side covers.

Danny took a Road King – a relatively small Bagger – and stripped it until it looked like a FXR, except that there aren't many FXRs with M-8 motors.

The ¾ rear view definitely looks like a FXR, but creating that appearance didn't come easily. First, Danny pulled off the rear subframe and made some mods to the frame itself. Next, he trimmed the length of a Road King Standard rear fender and reinforced the fender inside to provide enough support for the taillight and license assemblies.

Next, the fat gas tank had to go, replaced with an earlier, narrower, Road King tank. In order to make a tank that's not only narrow, but smooth across the top, the fuel pump access had to disappear. The answer was to cut out the bottom of a Sportster tank and weld it into the bottom of the new Road King tank (sounds simple, but ain't).

Anyone one who's up on the FXRs will know that the cop model (FXRP) had a few changes designed to make the bikes more appealing to the police departments. One of those changes was the bags. Instead of the clam-style bags we all know, the bags came as rectangular boxes protected by tubular mountings. The bags seen here are police reproductions from FXR Division, complete with mounts, but without the big hockey-puck releases in the top. Danny was able to bolt the mounts to the frame so they would be tucked in and help keep the bike nice and narrow.

For power, the hybrid FXR is powered with a Motorwitch special. A 129 cubic inch M-8 with a 4.5 inch S&S crankshaft and a pair of unique cylinders from Leading Edge with a 4.25 inch bore. The pistons are from Leading Edge as well, with a ratio of 11 to 1. The heads are Harley-Davidson Screamin' Eagle Stage 4 models. Breathing begins at the Arlen Ness air filter, then through the 62mm throttle body from HPI. The camshaft is a 550 from S&S and the two-into-one exhaust is from FAB 28. Behind the motor is a stock six-speed tranny, and chain drive to the rear wheel. Once on the dyno, the numbers showed that the combination of motor bits and pieces worked together. How about 144 horsepower and 155 for torque?

Like the rest of the bike, the suspension is made up of high-quality parts, like the complete fork assembly from Race Tech. Their design is meant for sport bikes, but Race Tech modified the specs

One unique motorcycle. Police bags and brackets, hand pounded side covers, the wrong gas tank, unique housing and a Rogue Rider Industries taillight.

Race Tech fork assembly, with radial mounts for the Brembo calipers. Wheel is another Carbon Fiber BST wheel, with a 19-inch Michelin Commander 3 tire.

The exhaust is from Wegner Racing, behind that is the Alloy Allow swingarm, supported by two Race Tech shocks.

There aren't many parts on this bike that Danny hasn't worked with – the motor is made up of 4.5-inch flywheels and two, 4.25-inch Leading Edge cylinders.

for the bike and Danny. Supported by the fork is a 19-inch Carbon Fiber wheel wrapped by a Michelin Commander 3 tire. Doing most of the slowing-down are two floating wave rotors and Brembo 4-piston calipers. In the rear, it's a case of another floating rotor and Brembo caliper. The rear wheel is an 18-inch Carbon wheel, again from BST. Of note, the front and rear wheels and tires are exactly the same size as those on the stock bike. As Danny explains,

"The Harley engineers probably spent hundreds of hours figuring exactly the best wheel and tire sizes for this Road King, so why use something else?"

Most of the components on this Road King/FXR are aftermarket components we've seen before. The headlight however, maybe not. This is a one-off design. The light itself is from Baja Designs LPG, they make lights for off-road race trucks. The nacelle is a Danny creation formed from aluminum.

The left side picture provides a good look at the unique Leading-Edge cylinders. Components in the primary are stock. Floorboards and pegs from H-D End Game.

Controls for the hands are genuine Harley-Davidson parts, the bars themselves are Split Angle T-Bars from FXR Division. The foot controls are from Harley-Davidson as well, though some came through the P&A Catalog.

Born Free is different from most shows, as Danny explains: "It's an invite-only show and H-D supplies the new bike to the builder. The bikes just go on display. In the case of the Street Road King - the bike was well received, and later was displayed at the H-D museum.

"As far as riding," Danny says, "It's great. It makes a lot of usable power with a nice linear delivery. Of all the bikes I've built over the years this one handles by far the best. My purpose was to shave the bike, build a bike that's light, narrow and handles well. I was able to get all those things accomplished - light, agile and truly a pleasure to ride."

Right: Danny set out to design a light, narrow motorcycle from the tall bars from FXR DIVISION to the tucked-in bags in back. A bike that's nimble and slides right through the traffic.

The final item in the driveline is the simple device called a 530 chain.

159 Cubic Inches

You could say Danny Wilson came by his mechanical and design skills from his male relatives. Grandfather was a mechanic and machinist who worked on race cars. His Dad earned his weekly check as a body man.

Though he grew up in California, he took up residence in Phoenix when he signed for training in MMI and used the skills to get a job working for a Harley dealership in Phoenix. Eventually he went to work for Harley-Davidson Corporate, helping owners overseas open and operate new dealerships in countries like Vietnam and Thailand. Responsibility included training the new crew, especially the techs. Danny picked-up his nickname of Motorwitch during his five years overseas. When one of the local newspapers wrote about the new Harley dealership, there were no words for "skilled motorcycle mechanic," and in their language, Denny was described as: the Motorwitch.

Once back in the US of A, Danny bounced around a bit, but the goal was a shop of his own. That came together when he moved into the FXR Division's building in north Phoenix. "I

The Road Glide 159 might be called a two-wheeled Buick with an aftermarket 500 cubic inch aftermarket engine. If he takes off hard when the light turns green, it either smokes the tire or picks up the front wheel. Danny's ideal was to build the biggest M-8, and I think he's achieved that goal.

named my new shop, the Leading Edge," explains Danny. "My goal was to design and build the components necessary to create the biggest displacement M-8 motors possible."

If you're going to design and manufacture new components, you need a test mule. In Danny's shop, the 2018 Road Glide is that test bed. One look at the bike and you see two things, the number 159 on the side cover, and the unusual cylinders with only four fins. Not a surprise that 159 is the cubic inches of the V-Twin. The surprise is the cylinders - his own design.

To get that 159, Danny installed a Leading Edge crankshaft with a 5 inch stroke and one-off connecting rods from CP Carrillo; and his unique cylinders, with a bore of 4.5 inches, and again, Carrillo made the special forged pistons. The cylinders of that size did require boring the cases to make room for the bigger spigots.

On top are ported Harley heads and motivating those four valves is a S&S 590 cam. Feeding the heads is a 70mm throttle body from HPJ. Bolted to the throttle body is an air cleaner from Screamin' Eagle. For exhaust, Danny picked a two-into-one system from Wegner Racing.

Over 200 horses running through the drive train requires a heavy-duty clutch from Evolution Industries clutch, and a Baker Grudge Box. From there the power goes to the rear wheel via a chain drive from Alloy Art, with a chain from EK Chain.

The unusual looking fork is a traditional assembly from Alloy Art. Bolted to the lower legs are two, Beringer, six-piston calipers. Bolted to the Harley front wheel is a pair of floating rotors from the same company.

Leading the bike is the 19-inch Harley wheel with a Dunlop tire. Supporting the wheel is a fork assembly from Alloy Art. Doing most of the stopping is the two, six-piston, calipers from Beringer.

This might be a big bike, but it's about as light as a Road Glide can be – due to the Carbon Fiber everywhere – fairing, front fender, dash, bags and side covers, all from Curtis Hofmann.

Left side shows off the floorboards from Flow Motorsports, the seat with the pocket for the rider is from Saddleman. Also, a good look at the Leading Edge cylinders with only four fins.

The wheel itself is a factory 19 inch rim with a Dunlop tire. The rear brake components are the ones from Milwaukee, as is the 18 inch wheel and another Dunlop tire. The stock swingarm went into the used-parts pile, replaced by the super-strong swingarm from Brock's. Supporting the ass-end of the Road Glide is a pair of two, Racing Brothers shocks (with gas).

Some test mules look rough after too much time working hard without a rest. Danny's mule, by contrast, looks pretty good. Nearly all the sheet metal components are from Hofmann, the exception piece is the Harley tank. All those Carbon Fiber pieces were painted in a nice deep red color, dark enough to show the red, but transparent enough that the fiber shows through. The one big

The tank is genuine steel from Milwaukee, painted black with an aftermarket red Carbon dash. All the Carbon parts are red – it's the "red weave."

piece that came from Harley was painted in glass-smooth black.

For the final assembly, Danny used a mix of Harley and aftermarket controls for the hands and feet. For example, the handlebars are from Vitty's, as are the adjustable risers. The controls on the ends of the handlebars are from Milwaukee. Floor-boards carry the FLO Motorsports logo. The license plate bracket and taillight are both from Alloy Art. Up front, the headlights are from Rogue Rider Industries. Finally, the seat is from Saddlemen.

Everyone wonders how an animal like this one behaves. According to Danny, "For as big as it is with that power output, it's actually pretty well mannered. With 5 inches of stroke I don't rev it past 6K, but it really never needs to go that high anyway. It delivers the power as soon as you twist the throttle, so you have to be ready for it when you do. As far as it being a day-to-day bike, and to be completely honest - it's not ideal for that. I explain that to customers who want a 159. It doesn't like being in traffic and doesn't like real hot days. It's great to ride on the open road and handles well under most conditions… and it sure is fun when you get after it. All in all, I'm very happy with the design and the performance."

Top:
Danny achieved the 159 cubics with a 5-inch stroker and a 4.5-inch pair of Danny's unique cylinders, all from Leading Edge. The rest of the motor is ported heads, a 70mm throttle body, a 590 camshaft and a two-into-one exhaust. On the dyno the motor registers 201 horsepower and 216 torque – not too bad.

Right:
Danny (Motorwitch) proving that the monster can be used as a regular bike, even in the city.

Cylinders

Leading Edge V-Twin

Most of us grew up believing that when it comes to cooling an air-cooled engine, more thin fins are better. Logic says that an abundant of thin fins presents more surface to the cool air.

Danny Wilson, however, took a fresh look at the issue. As he explains it:

"I looked at the motors on old, air-cooled aircraft - how the fins were spaced much farther apart than the tight-spacing we see now on all the air-cooled motorcycles. That piqued my curiosity, and eventually I came up with my design. There are only 4 Fins on the cylinders, and the surface between the fins is rough and you can see the machining marks. The large span between the fins creates tunnels for air movement. If you look closely at the surface, you will note there are high and low spots, and tool marks. The uneven surface creates air disturbance as it runs over the surface – the rough surface makes it easier for the air to pull the heat from the surface."

Danny's unique cylinders are made from billet aluminum with ductile iron liners. The current catalog includes kits that start at 125 cubic inches and go all the way to 159 inches for M-8s. The two smallest kits, the 125 and 129 inches, are designed for an installation in 107 and 114 inch - while the cases stay in the frame. The rest of the kits are aimed at the more serious enthusiasts. These kits include cylinders and a crankshaft and start at 131 cubic inches and go right up to 159 inches. Similar cylinders and kits will soon be available for Twin Cams.

Leading Edge V-Twin
1221 W. Pierce St.
Phoenix Arizona 85007
Shop phone 602-399-4617
motorwitchcylinders

Chapter 13

Trask

Assault Bikes

Q & A with Nick Trask

Assault bikes are the creation of Nick Trask and each Assault is numbered. Though they are similar to each other, each is unique for the owner. In order to understand the Assault I've interviewed the man who dreamed up the Assault.

Give me just a little background, how did you pick turbos? A lot of people have developed and sold turbos, but nobody ever made a good business out of turbos. So you've figured out something somebody else hasn't.

Everywhere else in the world you can't afford the gas, so all the motors are small, right? But take a little motor, just add a turbo charger, and it will make up the missing power. And its dependable power, it comes on gradually. Almost like a rubber band. The hit isn't harsh, it doesn't shock the drive line, it sneaks up on the drive line smoothly. I prefer the turbo to a blower. That's why we went for it. No one was doing it. No one was doing it correctly. And I had a background, I had experience with turbos, so I went ahead with my idea.

How long have you been at this? Almost 20 years.

Did you have this in your head when you came over? Just yesterday a guy asked, 'Look, did you know at the beginning that you'd be here today'? And I said, 'No. I was green, I was as green as they come. I had no idea. But you just

Mr. Trask, the one who made a business out of Turbos, and then used the Turbo to create the Assault concept.

never give up and you're always going forward. And don't look behind you. And you'll get there - or you get somewhere. You can't sit still.'

Hopefully it's somewhere in the direction that you wanna be. We built a hell of a company, and we have a product line that's desirable. Guys want it. I can't sell something I don't like. We've gone through a lot of growing pains, stages maybe. When you come up with problems, you have to overcome the problems and move on. If you keep moving, you make

Built in limited numbers, an Assault starts life as Road King with a little 107 motor with no fairing and nothing to settle it from any other Road Kings. A few months later that no-name child has a respected pedigree.

a better product. Our systems are bolt-on. We'll go to Sturgis and install 30 turbos on motorcycles during Sturgis. And those guys come from all over the country. And we've been doing that for probably 12 years.

You always have a booth in Sturgis, you probably come home from Sturgis with money in your pocket and a list of people to call. But I'm thinking the booth is a lot of work and expense. So, there must be more to it than just the money? Yes, there is more than

The finished motorcycle is about as fast as any bikes on the road. From the front to the back, the components are high quality. Almost all the "sheet metal parts" are actually Carbon Fiber – including the front fender, fairing, dash, side covers, bags and rear fender.

money. We are there partly to support the industry and keep it exciting. We help our customers who need it; and give them something to look forward to. Something to be excited for, so they don't go out and buy Jet Skis, right? Keep the industry alive. We all support each-other, and it doesn't matter if you get something now or not. You've gotta jump in and you gotta be part of it. Yeah, that's been my motto since day one - and it's worth it.

Some say we don't need these motorcycles. We don't need to make 'em go faster. But we do want to make them bigger, stronger and badder. That's what we do here at Trask. We try to make killer parts and killer motorcycles that guys can feel proud of when they open the box and put the parts on their bike. They feel proud that it's a genuine Trask product. It's made in the U.S. and it's unique.

From the beginning we worked to design a kit that somebody, like a mechanical guy, can put together at their garage. He doesn't have to take it to a shop. All of our turbo kits are 100% bolt-on. That average guy can put it on their bike in his garage with basic tools. If a

The heart of an Assault is the motor – approximately 180 horsepower pushing a bike to a speed sometimes limited only by the jockey. The Turbo V-Twin is beautiful both inside and outside. Heads ported from Ward, larger aftermarket throttle body, injectors with capacity for more fuel, and as a result – more and more power.

The Trask Calipers hold four-pistons, mounted on the radial style mount on the lower part of the inverted fork legs from Ohlins. Interesting, the spacer between the caliper and the mount, is also the support bracket for the Carbon fender.

Hand controls came with the bike, the risers and handlebars however are Trask creations. The Carbon Dash across the tank is another Trask product.

customer has a question or an issue, we answer the phones here and help them, and walk them through whatever stage of the assembly they're at, and make sure it's done correctly. We want to be sure that they're satisfied with our product.

What do you do for the fuel and ignition curves? We use Thundermax, a Thundermax computer. We've worked with Jerry for 11 years and we get what we need. We get our tables built into the system. We have boost fuel-enrichment, and we retard timing during boost. We went so far as to have our own sensor made. It's the right deal. After the installation you can't even tell. A lot of times you put on a super charger or whatever, there's usually a little spot in the tune-up that's not right. And you compromise. With our system, you put it on and it's like a stock bike, runs great, just a lot faster. You bolt on the turbo and go. And it'll do an automatic auto-tune from our base map.

We've got these things dialed in now. We've done so many of 'em. We ship 'em all over the world and they work.

The floorboards are another Trask item. Inside the primary housing is a stock H-D chain and clutch basket with aftermarket discs. The tranny is makeup of aftermarket gears and shafts, transfers the power to the rear wheel via a 530 chain.

In the shop, the early days of construction. Frame is pretty bare here, Trask subframe in place, along with the Trask swingarm.

Making progress, the new motor is placed into the frame, along with the primary components and the chain drive. Up front, the fairing is assembled, along with the risers and handlebars.

Floorboards and pegs are in place, missing the gas tank, dash, front fender and plenty of wiring and hoses.

The Nuts and Bolts of the Assault – by Moots

If one man dreamed up the Assault (and other go-fast parts), another man – Moots - made sure those ideas came to life. Moots is the man with a wide range of responsibilities at Trask. In the morning he might be in the shop assembling an Assault or working on a customer's bike. In the afternoon he's likely in the office ordering parts or helping a customer. He's also the manager of the Trask Race Team.

Q&A with Moots

Tell us about the Assault bike? Tell us what the idea was, how, where did the idea come from. The Assault bike was part of the transition from our sport bikes to sport Baggers. People are setting their Baggers up for sport riding, going hard into turns, making lots of power. We are building the bikes with the proper components to enhance their ability to do so. The original idea came from Nick. Nick is a very creative man.

What do you start with to build an Assault? We start with a stock Bagger, a Road King. Then we change out all the body parts, except for the fuel tank, to Carbon Fiber. We drop the weight quite a bit. Then we install our components, like the billet rear section and swingarm, that takes another 28 pounds off. Then we proceed to install quality suspension; Ohlins front suspension, Trask swingarm, Legend rear shocks, and we set all of them for the rider's weight.

Moots – the man who wears many hats, from shop manager to hands-on mechanic.

So, they're not all exactly the same? They're all pretty much the same except for a few things, like the actual suspension settings. We tune each one to the rider.

The parts with the Trask logo are manufactured in the Trask building in North Phoenix by Trask employees.

Tell me more about the motor. The motor usually starts as a 107. The original bike is a base model bike. We take the motor all the way down to bare cases. We put in a S&S or a Darkhorse crankshaft, depending on the customer's choice. And, bump it up to a 124, 128 or 131 inch motor, depending on the customer's choice. On the Assault Series, we've been using the S&S kit that comes with a 550 cam. We install our big turbo, the Assault Turbo Kit.

What do you get for horsepower? The 128s are pushing about 210 horses on pump gas with eight to eight-and-a-half pounds of boost.

Anything else that I should know about those motors? We also have the heads done. The heads are done by Ward Performance, and we've had some of the heads done by Fuel Moto. We run a large throttle body, usually a Screamin' Eagle 64 millimeter.

Tell us about the suspension, starting on the front? It's an Ohlin inverted front end, which is a much more stable, with less unsprung weight, than the factory fork. And the internal valving is much more specific than the stock Harley setup.

In the back, we use Legend shocks with a remote canister of nitrogen. These are adjustable for preload and dampening, extension dampening and compression dampening - it just allows us to manipulate the settings to give the rider what he needs.

Anything else you want to add? Well, the bikes are ergonomically correct for each rider. The bikes are very nimble, they're a lot of fun to ride - and no shortage of power!

At Trask you make and sell more than just Turbo Kits and Assault bikes? Yes. Our catalog of aftermarket parts is growing. We have exhaust systems, high-flow

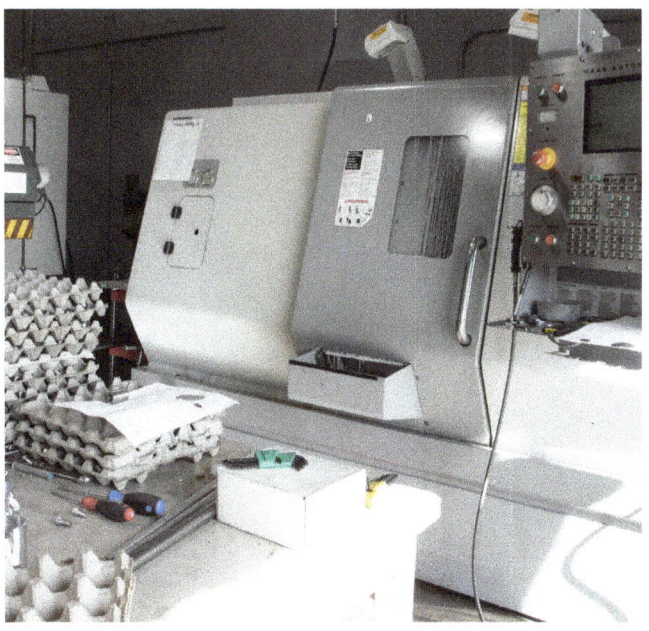

This is just one of the many Trask CNCs – makes it easy to create a new test-part. And if the new product passes all the day-to-day tests, the CNCs will crank out the real part – a new item for the Trask catalog.

The Trask racer might be called an Assault on speed. More power and fewer parts necessary for the street.

For the race rules, the Trask bike is limited to 107 cubic inches – because they get to run their Turbo. A crankshaft assembly from Darkhorse with a stock stroke of 4.375 inch stroke, and the cylinders measure 3.937 inches. Camshaft is a one-off Trask camshaft, heads ported by Rick Ward, and the throttle body of 64mm.

The racer bike is taller than an Assault, so the bags don't drag. Brakes are from Beringer, both the four-piston calipers and the rotors for front and rear. Wheels are aluminum, 17 inches both front and rear, 120/70 up front and 180/60 in the rear, tire brands depend on the racetrack.

air cleaner, swingarms, risers, cam covers with a window. We manufacture nearly all our Trask parts. Everything starts as an idea, then a drawing and then it becomes a concept. We have our R&D Department, and a full machine shop with a row of CNCs. We make a test part and then it goes through rigorous testing and fitment. We make sure the products do what they're supposed to do. Only then we put them in production and in our catalog.

What about the Racing Bikes, how did you guys get into the racing? As soon as the Bagger Racing thing was invented, they approached us to see if we, you know, we're interested. And, Nick just jumped all over it.

What do you start with to build a race bike? It's based on our Assault bike, but it's much more stripped down. We remove all of the internals from the fairing. We, eliminate a good portion of the wiring harness and just try to lighten it any way that we possibly can. Our race bike is also a water-cooled motor, as opposed to air and oil-cooled. Which is because of the stress that it goes through in the course of a race.

How big is the race bike, other than the water, what do you use to get more horsepower? For the races we're legally restricted to a 107 cubic inches, because we're running a Turbo. We run it at 14 pounds of boost. We run it on race fuel. That allows us to achieve the horsepower necessary to compete with the big inch motors that are out there.

Trask has been running a Race bike from the beginning of Bagger, and done pretty well with winning and getting second or third.

Nick Trask and three guys who helped him succeed at the race.

Chapter 14
Joe

The Beast

As they say: If you don't get it right the first time, just try again. In the case of Joe's 2019 Road Glide, the bike is really the second attempt at building the perfect Bagger.

It all started with the 2018 Road Glide Joe purchased and proceeded to make it into a hot rod – with help from Randy Cramer. What came as a 114-inch stock Harley M-8, became a 128 inch M-8 shortly after the purchase. As most knowledgeable riders know, the easiest way to get more cubes is to install bigger cylinders (but not so big that the cases must be machined) and matching pistons. It's a relatively simple operation, and the work is usually done with the motor in the frame. And like most bikers, Joe wanted the right cams, and ported heads to accompany the extra cubic – and to a good tune on the dyno. Chassis-wise, Randy swapped out the forks and the shocks for quality aftermarket components and did the same with the brakes.

Now, most riders would be more than satisfied with the 2018, but Joe isn't like most riders.

As Randy Cramer recalls, "about a year later, Joe dropped off another Road Glide, a 2019 Road

What was a nice, stock Road Glide became a Beast – in the hands of Rick Ward and Randy Cramer.

Glide with 50 miles on the odometer. Joe said he wanted a monster motor. While he was in the shop Joe and I talked about putting a fat tire on the front. When he left, it was set – one monster motor and one fat tire. Of course, he wanted the aftermarket chassis and brakes, along with a few goodies. In the end, Joe leaves it to me – he just says – 'buy the best.'"

When Joe dropped the 2019 Road Glide off at Randy's shop, he insisted on a monster motor - that was at the top of his list. Rather than take this the motor apart in the shop, Randy pulled it out of the bike and shipped it to Rick Ward where the displacement made a big jump from 114 to 143 cubic inches.

To make a 143, you need a 4.5-inch stroke and 4.5-inch bore. The big cylinders meant boring

The first think Randy did was to pull out the motor, and ship it to Rick Ward's shop. Soon that 114 inch V-Twin was nothing but a pile of parts. Set aside was the crankshaft, replaced with a Darkhorse replaced with a 4.5 inch crank. Next, Rick bored the cylinder to the same dimension, and the two new numbers makes a 143 cubic inch Motor.

the cases to make room for the cylinder's spigots – which of course means a complete disassembly. Rick Ward ordered custom ductile iron sleeves and used them to sleeve the stock M-8 cylinders, to a bore of 4.5 inches. The boring and honing wasn't done until the cylinders fit a pair of custom forged pistons from CP-Carrillo. For a crank, he chose an assembly from Darkhorse.

In the breathing department, Rick started with a Zippers air cleaner feeding a ported H-D SE throttle body, bolted to a pair of Wards Heads. Of course, those heads are ported and equipped with oversize valves.

Because Joe wanted a big front tire, the Carbon wheel is 5.5 X 18 inches with a Dunlop Sport tire. The new four-piston calipers are from Brembo matched to rotors from Lyndall.

On the right switches are from Milwaukee, and the master cylinder is from Beringer.

Where there's a primary housing there's usually the double chain - here there's a belt drive and a clutch assembly from BDL.

For a tranny, Randy chose another Grudge Box from Baker. And a monster motor requires more than a heavy-duty transmission – like a heavy-duty clutch driven by a BDL primary belt drive. From the clutch the power goes through the Baker Box and from there to the rear wheel via the chain drive from Zippers.

The rear suspension is pretty simple. Shocks from Ohlins H-D 044 are supporting Brock's tubular aluminum swingarm, which in turn are supporting the BST Carbon wheel — a wheel just as light as it is strong. Up front, Randy set the stock fork assembly aside, and replaced it with a complete assembly from Kraus/Ohlins. Bolted to the BST front wheel are the rotors from Lyndall, coupled to Brembo 484-108mm four-piston calipers.

Because Joe wanted a big fat rubber up front, both wheels are essentially the same size – 5.5 X 18 inches. Tires are likewise the same sizes – 180/165-18 inches. By the way, don't try to buy a fat Carbon Fiber front wheel from Brock, Joe's was a special order.

Wrapping that fat front tire is a steel fender from Native Customs, and a Carbon Fiber rear fender from Curtis Hofmann. Mounted on either side of the rear fender are a pair of Curtis' saddle bags and the side covers. At the very front there's the biggest Carbon item on the bike – the fairing, simply left with their weave showing through the clear.

Joe is now the owner of two, very fast, very cool, Road Glide Performance Baggers. As he explains about the 2019, "It's the only fat tire/Carbon front wheel that I've seen. The two bikes are similar to ride. They both handle great, but I can ride the '18 through the canyon a little faster, 'cause it's a little lighter in the front end with the smaller tire. On the other hand, when I ride the '19 you need to be really careful. You twist the throttle and if there's any dirt on the asphalt, I mean anything, you're all over. On hard-packed clean asphalt it wants to stand up – that's what happens with 230 horses. Yes, the '19 is a beast."

From this angle it's easy to see the single-row 530 chain driving the 5.5X18 inch Carbon rear wheel and Dunlop tire – all of it connected to the aluminum swingarm from Brocks, and the swingarm is supported by two shocks from Ohlins.

Handlebar is from L.A. Chopper, mirrors are from Ness, in the back you see the reservoir containers for the shocks.

The fairing, bags, side covers and rear fender are all Hofmann's Carbon Fiber body parts (the grey is the color of the weave). Front fender is from Native Customs. The inverted fork is another Ohlins/Kraus combination.

The Sleeper

Joe Duenser is a man blessed with an oversize shop filled with motorcycles. One of those is a 2016 Street Glide, a black and white plain-Jane of a bike. What we used to call a sleeper.

"Right after I bought it," says Joe, "I took it to a shop in Denver and the builder there put in a 143-inch motor from S&S. I had some problems with that motor, and I'm partly at fault. In the end I took it to Randy Cramer, and he turned it into a 148-inch motor"

Randy pulled the motor apart, and instead of a simple overhaul, he used the cases as the foundation for one hot Twin Cam. A 143 inch V-twin is big, but Randy figured that too many cubes is almost enough. So, he started with two fresh cylinders from S&S and bored them to 4.455 inches. The pistons and con-rods came from CP. For the bottom-end Randy ordered a complete crank from Darkhorse with a 4.5 inch stoke, for a total of 148 cubic inches.

Seems most of the really kick-ass Baggers are Road Glide. Joe's FLHRX (Street Glide) is an exception. Most of the stock components are gone, replaced with nothing but the very best, installed by Randy Cramer.

Randy chose B3, high-performance heads from S&S, and cams with .635 inch lift, coupled to 1.75:1 rocker arms lift, for a total lift of .674 inches. To ensure that those wide-open intake ports have enough air Randy chose a 64mm throttle body from HPI and an air cleaner from Zipper. To use a cliché, what goes in must come out - the exhaust in this case is a combo pipe and muffler from S&S and D&D.

To make serious power it takes more than just bolting together well-known parts. All those cams and valves and pistons have to work together - timing is everything. When it all does work together it's a beautiful thing, synergy (when two plus two equals five). In this case it means 148 cubic inches means 196 horses on the Dyno.

This sleeper Street Glide is all about motor, but of course all that power has to get to the street via the primary, clutch, tranny and final drive. All Joe's horses go through a primary chain, a heavy-duty clutch assembly, and a Baker Grudge Box. The last link in the chain of power is a number 530.

So, we have a killer motor and drive line, what about the suspension? It's more of the best of best of course. At the front, Randy installed the inverted fork legs from Ohlins, clamped in triple trees from Kraus. Mounted in that front end is a 19 by 3-inch Carbon wheel from Brock. Bolted to the hub are two rotors from Lyndall, matched to two 484-108 calipers from Brembo.

In the back, that name Brock comes up twice. First, there's a 18X5.5-inch Carbon wheel supported by a competition swingarm that's both light and strong, (and makes it possible to stretch the wheelbase three

Small batwing fairing and trimmed front fender make for a compact motorcycle – with a Day Maker headlight.

What started as a 143 inch V-Twin is now a 148 cubic inch motor (too much is almost enough). Cylinder heads are B3s ffrom S&S, cylinders bored to 4.455 inches. Inside the H-D cases is the 4.5 inch crankshaft from Darkhorse.

The front wheel is 3.0 X 19 inches with Ceramic Bearings. Calipers are from Beringers with rotors from Lyndall.

inches). Supporting that swingarm is a pair of two H-D O44 shocks from Legends.

When Joe plans a new bike, aesthetics are not at the top of the list. He's happy with a machine that's just clean and simple. Thus, the parts like the fenders and bags from Curtis Hofmann were left in the Carbon Fiber finish, while the tank and fairing were painted black and white. Ten-inch handlebars are higher than the stockers, but still leave Joe hands behind the faring and out of the breeze on cool rides. Master cylinders are both from Beringer. the Butcher floor-boards are from Twisted Choppers.

The black and white street glide is one of Joe's famous daily riders - just a sleeper that surprises riders on the street. Some guys pull up with a hot bike street thinking, "I can kick this guy's ass." They should think again, because the Street Glide has 200 horses. Just as important is the pilot - and Joe simply never loses. Never.

Helping that 148-inch motor make almost 200 horses is that long, two-into-one exhaust assembled from D&D and S&S parts. Bags and the rear fender are Carbon Fiber parts from Hofmann Design.

The primary cover houses double-wide chain and a heavy-duty clutch assembly. The final link to the rear wheel – 18X5.5 Carbon Fiber - is a 530-chain kit from Zippers.

Another case of stock switches, mirrors from the Ness catalog and a Beringer master cylinder for the calipers…

… the dash is stock, the handlebar is from L. A. Choppers, only 10 inches high.

Q&A with Joe Duenser

Give us some background on you and your involvement with motorcycles. I've been involved with motorcycles for 44 years. I bought my first brand new Harley in 1984 and I still own it. A few years later I bought an 1988 FLH, I still own that too. Then and now, I just never leave nothin' stock (laughs). All the way back in the '80s, we were puttin' stroker motors in 'em and hoppin' 'em up. A little later we were puttin' fat tires on the front of FXRs.

Do you work on the bikes, on the builds? I'm not a bike builder (laughs). I'm a demolition and concrete contractor. I know a hell of a lot more about that, than I do about building the bikes. I just enjoy the hell out of 'em. And I like doing the projects, being a part of each project.

How many bikes do you own? 18 bikes right now. Um, we're going back to a 1908 Indian, all the way through my stuff that I have today. You know, I own some Panheads, a Knucklehead with a side car and factory reverse, four FXRs. I have a '84 FXSB that I bought brand new in '84. It was the last year of the Shovel, first year of the belt drive. I have all kinda stuff, like a Ducati Panigale V-4-R.

How did you get involved with Performance Baggers, and Randy Cramer? Like I said, six

Joe was making Performance Baggers way before anyone even thought of that label. He simply likes Baggers for long trips with a measure of comfort, and he likes to get there quickly – very quickly.

months after I bought the 1988 FLH, I put a stroker kit in it and a BDL open primary, after that I had Dick Scully do a flamed custom paint job. Hot rod Baggers are in my blood. I like the long-distance capabilities of the Baggers, but I also must have the performance. Like I said, I still own that FLH bike and it's the favorite of all my motorcycles - just because it has so much history with me.

As far as Randy Cramer goes; a friend of mine had a problem during Sturgis some years back. We were in Spearfish and we found a shop there. I went in and introduced myself to the owner - Randy. I really liked the guy. So I've done business with him over the years, quite a bit of business. He doesn't BS you. Everything he does, he does it right, he's conscientious about his product. Randy's the most honest person I've ever met.

We photographed two bikes from your collection. One is a Street Glide with a 148 Twin Cam motor, and the other a Road Glide with a 143 M-8 motor. Can you talk about those two bikes? Well, the Street Glide, It's set up as good as you can set that bike up. It's got Carbon Fiber wheels, Carbon body parts, a Darkhorse crank in the motor. It's got the all-in suspension, the inverted fork, Brembo brakes. From top to bottom, it's a Performance Bagger.

I have two Road Glides. I built an '18 with the 128 motor. And it's the perfect motorcycle, the best suspension and all the rest. So, I wanted to build a bigger inch motor and Randy kinda talked me into the fat tire on the front. I like it a lot. Um, I'm a little more of a fan of the narrower tire for the canyons. But it handles great. It runs, it's a beast.

With the Road Glide with the 143 motor you gotta be really careful. You twist the throttle, and, if there's even a little bit on the asphalt – anything - you're all over. On hard-packed asphalt it goes straight toward the sky, you know?

What's the biggest different between the Steet Glide and Road Glide? In my opinion the Road Glides are just a little better to make into performance bikes. Just because they don't have that batwing fairing. Aerodynamically, Road Glides work a little better. That Street Glide, though, it's a great bike, I don't ride it near as much as the Road Glides.

Here's a guy who's not exactly a youngster, who rides all the time …

… and his trips aren't just up-to the local bar and then back home. More like Denver to Phoenix for example.

He's been known to race as well, not a drag race, more like from Sturgis to Deadwood. Rumor has it he's never lost.

Chapter 15
D&D

Sometimes you're just wandering along under the Sturgis sun, and all of a sudden, WOW, it's raining. If you're walking along Main Street, the rain is just an excuse to stop in the one of the bars and have a cold one. So what if it's only 9:00 AM? If you're one of the thousands walking through a vendor area, at Sturgis H-D, there are plenty of tents to tuck under. I did that very thing and as I looked out I realized the D&D Road King was sitting in the rain – the big rain drops and puddles made for some interesting pics.

The D&D booth was jammed with customer bikes, and Rusty couldn't find a place to hide his personal bike from the rain.

A very nice ride. Bright red with just enough chrome to make it stand out.

The classic Harley front fender, along with a PM four-piston chrome calipers, and rotors. Calipers mounted on the radial-style mount.

Behind the Screamin' Eagle air cleaner there's a 128 inch M-8 with a S&S crankshaft and ported heads.

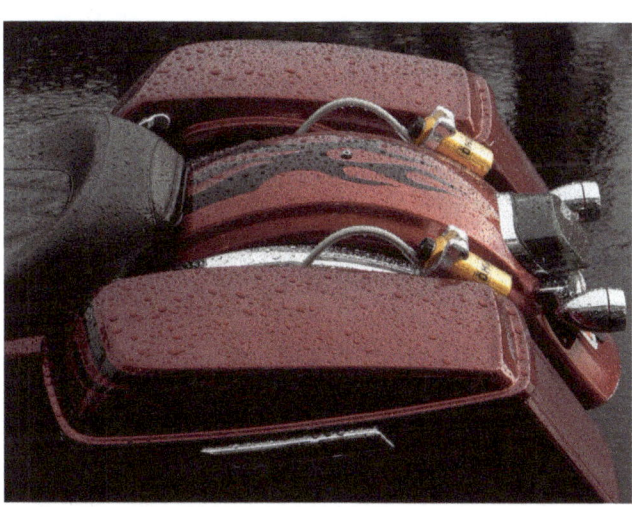

The Bags are stock, the piggy-back reservoirs from Ohlins shocks are mounted between bag and fender.

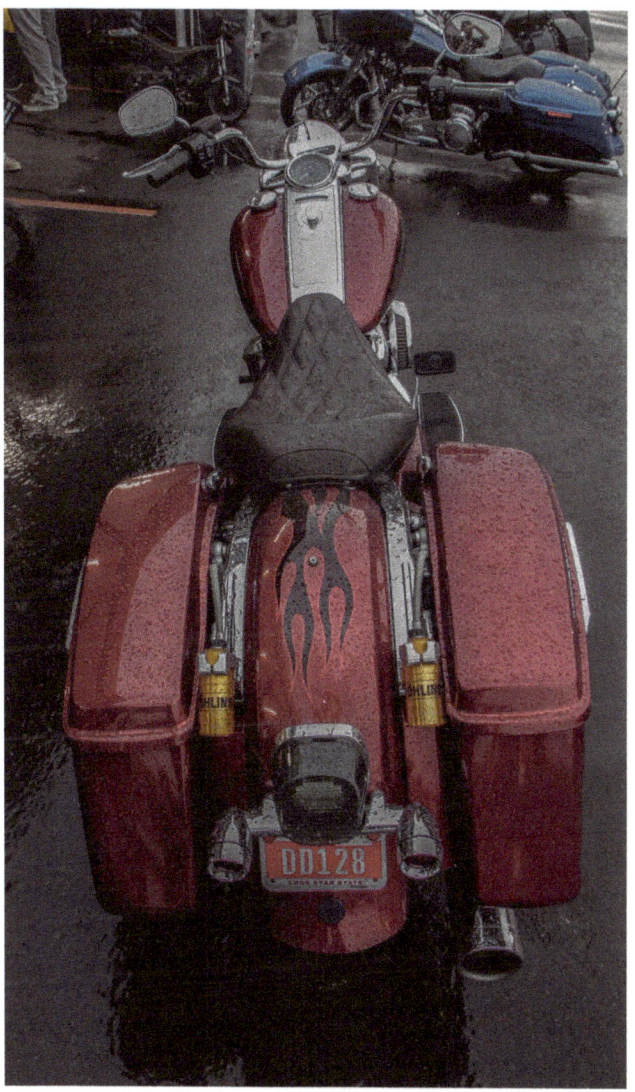

Rear view shows the aftermarket slanted taillight, and chrome LEDs for brake/turn lights.

Chapter 16

Pipes

Written by Pipes Gilliland

As we all know, in today's world of motorcycles, Performance Baggers are damned popular. I personally have a different take on what this should mean. I believe a road-touring, Performance Bagger needs more than horsepower and big brakes. The bike should have style, stance, and hidden features only a trained eye can see. A bike should be a convertible - the ability to throw the tour-pac on and go for a 1000 mile trip in comfort as well.

This build started as a base 2018 Road King, with all the typical Harley crap, some parts were chrome, some of it black, fasteners are cadmium plated? The bikes come with "Bagger" suspension as usual. Comfortable on a touring ride around the lake. Dive it into a corner, however, what happens? The same bikes have a Bagger wobble at high speeds and oil carry-over problems in the primary,

So, if I'm to build a real machine, that requires a total tear down.

The Ford blue Bagger doesn't look like all the other Baggers. but that doesn't mean it isn't fast.

The M-8 power plant was first, we took it completely down to the crank, and took the crank to Revolution Performance for a complete truing and balancing of the assembly.

I elected one of my great friends, and NHRA professional, Deric Churchill of DC V TWIN to help with piston and cam design, along with the porting of the heads. My goal was to build a 117-cu. in. V-twin, one of my favorite combinations. We used 4.125 pistons and 4.374 inches for the stroke, a big enough motor that's reliable, runs on pump gas and turns good numbers on the dyno.

When it was time to deal with the heads, Deric started with Kibblewhite components. Valves machined out of forged stainless, and guides made in their facility from bronze. Springs start as ground chrome Silicone wire. Before packaging them, springs are heat treated, shot peened and x-rayed. Seats are manufactured from powdered metal. They make their own seals from Viton, durable and resistance to heat. Holding the whole affair together, the titanium retainers, both light and very tough. Deric did the porting; the valves are 1.90 and 1.630 inches for intake and exhaust.

The assembly started with the fresh crank assembly, followed by pistons with rings and pin retainers. Cylinders are next, followed by the ported heads and 555 cams camshaft custom by redshift, and S&S camplate. I specified roller rockers and secondary breathers in the rocker covers.

A Horsepower 62 mm throttle body was attached with 5.5 gram per second injectors. A D&D 2-into-1 exhaust with billet

With the small fairing it becomes a Café bike. Brakes are H-D Calipers and Galfer rotors. Wheel is made from Carbon, 19X3 wrapped with a Dunlop 130/60/19.

Only 117 cubic inches, but with 10.8 to 1 compression, all new internals, a 555 DC V Twin cam, and ported with 1.90- and 1.63-inch valves, and a 62mm throttle body - the motor hit 149 horses on the dyno.

In the primary housing is the factory chain and a clutch from DC V Twin Custom.

cap, and false left pipe. This was selected after many runs with various pipes, The D&D works extremely well with this combination.

The gearbox was sent to Mark at R&D Transmission in Florida for a full treatment. That includes back-cut new after-market gears and a coating of Nitrate to the gears and shafts to minimize friction (each gear is rockwelled, so hardness of each gear is the same, allows gears to flex under power and not break).

Next, due to the issues with Harley's oil carryover issues in the primary and transmission, I designed a trap and vent which was installed on the outer primary. This allows the primary to also Vent, eliminating more friction loss thru the drive. Then I contacted my good friend Nick Trask and acquired his newly developed transmission top cover with a vent. This piece was developed on the Bagger Road race series.

To put this power to the ground I picked a Diamond Terminator clutch from Evolution Industry V-Twin billet clutch basket, with lockup and ceramic clutch plates. These plates allow me to let it slip when I twist the throttle and let go the clutch. The plates lock up with the build of horsepower and throttle.

Out back, I used Brock's performance pro street swingarm, to stabilize the rear of the bike, with help from the Ohlins Blackline shocks, they're fully adjustable to control the ride. The custom rear pully is machined and Hydro-dipped to match Brock's Performance blue ink carbon fiber wheels. Yes, I did order Carbon Fiber wheels, and I ordered them with ceramic bearings - 19-inch front and 18-inch in the rear. Dunlop tires installed for grip. Up front, I used Ohlins fork legs, you can change the front springs and

Café fairing, long front fender, paint design and thin seat work together to create Pipes' stance.

dampeners to correct the stance and handling of the front end.

I wanted an aggressive look and stance, and I tried different looks. I chose a Memphis Shades front fairing, and I modified the mount, so the bike has the looks and stance I was after. A set of Nick Trask's Moto bars seemed ideal, after I modified the bars and positioned the hand controls to get the profile correct. The end result gives me the aggressive sitting position I love on a fast bike.

The seat, as you notice, has been cut down. I designed it myself for fitment. Once I had the foam cut to my liking, I sent it to Tyler's shop, Smith Customs of Cross Lanes, West Virginia, they're known for magic hot rod interiors and bike seats. My finished seat provides good support under hard pulls, wheelies and drag racing, and still has a certain style. The seat is also built to match the detachable tour pack.

Next, we took all these parts: Inner and outer primary, cam cover, rocker boxes, pushrod tubes, clutch cover, transmission covers and the swingarm, and had them had polished. Then coated the parts with gloss-black

Handlebars are from Trask. The grips, mirrors, and hand controls are all from Harley-Davidson.

The convertible Bagger. It's a hot café racer one minute, and a touring machine with the add of the tour pac.

powder by Millers Powder Coating in Southern Georgia.

Paint work was done by Johnstons Bike and Body Works, along with my great friend Darin Allen for pinstriping. Colors are done in Ford Mustang Boss Blue, with Vivid black and orange. All PPG Concept paint, including the 2021 clear.

Now, it was Dyno time. I like to do the tuning at DC V Twin, using the TTS tuning system. However, before we put it on the dyno, I had to pick a low-profile air cleaner, one that wouldn't choke the motor. The Screamin' Eagle Ventilator air cleaner had a low profile and looked aggressive, However, when we started tuning on the dyno, we found a chunk of horsepower was missing. I went back to my shop, reworked the backing plate, spaced the outer cover, installed a venturi, and added a larger K&N filter, then, dyno again.

Then we were workin'. Final numbers - 149.92 horsepower and 139 foot-pounds of torque. Keep in mind the fact we run on pump gas, and the motor is only 117 cubic inches, smaller than most of the hot rod Baggers.

In the end, I ended with a bike that's a blast to ride with plenty of power with the ability to put the power on the ground. And Loud? Yes! I come-by my nickname honestly.

Top: The final drive to the rear wheel is a Kevlar belt. Brock's Performance Pro Street Swingarm supported by Ohlins shocks.

Center: This is the Screamin' Eagle air filter, modified and improved by Pipes.

Bottom: Pipes tends to think outside of the box, he's been doing it for years and will likely continue building fast bikes that look just a little different than the others.

Chapter 17
A Skunk on the Loose

Like a lot of bike owners, Chaz came up against one tough decision: to keep the current bike or buy a brand-new motorcycle? "At about the bike's fifth year," Chaz recalls, "I started thinking; buy a new Road Glide, or customize and hop up the Road Glide I already own?"

As the pictures show, Chaz took the more difficult road, pull the 2015 Road Glide down to the bare frame, and start over.

At the start of the project, Chaz had to make another decision: whether to do the bulk of the mechanical in his own garage, with his own hands. Or take it to a reputable bike builder and let him do all the work in his shop.

Randy Cramer is the builder he chose. As Chaz explained, "He's built other bikes for me, and he has a really good reputation with a group of very persnickety group of riders."

Chaz's to-do list started with the suspension. "I knew the original suspension was worn, so Randy and I decided to install Legend's Revo shocks in the back. Up front, instead of buying a

This is a case of "overhaul." Instead of walking in to the dealership and signing the contract with the amount of the payments, Chaz took his 2015 Bagger and decided to overhaul the machine, with a friend, and without borrowing any cash.

Handlebars are 10 inch Modular models. The Dash came from Hofmann's warehouse.

complete inverted fork assembly, we disassembled the stock forks and installed Legend Axios Cartridges for the forks."

While they were working on the suspension, it seemed a good time to buy some wheels. As Chaz explains the decision, "When I put together a plan for the overhaul of my old bike, I realized that good performance relies on more than just a big motor. Brock's Carbon Fiber wheels makes an amazing difference in the handling, as well as the acceleration and deceleration – so I told Randy to order two of the BST wheels."

The last suspension item on the list was a swingarm, and it was Randy who decided we should buy from Brock, as Randy explains, "Seems like everyone has a swingarm for sale now, but Brock was the first. I like to stay with the person who came up with an idea and did the testing and improving to make it a really good product. Brock's swingarm requires a mounting bracket, and I install so many of those swingarms I designed and manufacture my own bracket."

While they were at it, Randy and Chaz put in another order for additional Carbon Fiber components. In this case, they ordered a front and rear fender and a dash from Curtis Hofmann. Altogether, those shaved off a considerable amount of weight. Chaz felt that taking off weight would improve the bike's performance in every part of the riding experience – he went so far to insist on a Lithium battery with a weight of three pounds.

To slow down the reborn Road Glide, Randy suggested Galfer, 13-inch wave rotors, squeezed by Brembo 484, 108MM calipers from Kraus Motor Co.- two up front and one in back. To control those calipers, Randy and Chaz decided to buy from

A nice clean Bagger, with taillights that are tucked in. Note the Swingarm from Brocks, and the BST rear 5.5X18 wheel. Hidden behind the Bags are the Legends Revos shocks.

a company with an OK reputation – Harley-Davidson.

When it comes to building motors, each builder seems to have his or her recipe. For a 103 Twin Cam, Randy has his own. The most important part of that recipe is the cylinders and pistons.

Randy starts with new cylinders, and bores them out to 3.937 inches, instead of the stock 3.875. Fitted to the new cylinders are forged 10.8-to-one pistons from CP, connected to the crank with stock H-D connecting rods. The net effect of the bored cylinders is a 107 cubic inch Twin Cam.

The crank made a trip to Darkhorse where they were welded, trued and balanced. The stroke of 4.375 was left alone. To ensure the crank is well supported and prevented from moving side to side, Randy installed Timken bearings in the left-side case. Sealing off the cylinders and make good breathing, is a pair of heads from Rick Ward. Operating those valves are two 594 cams from Feuling.

The air for Chaz' new/old Bagger starts at the Trask air cleaner, then slides through a Screamin' Eagle 58mm throttle body, and past the intake valves. After the power cycle, the spent exhaust makes it past those other vales and to the atmosphere via a two-into-one exhaust. When all was done and Randy could strap it to the Dyno,

Calipers are from Brembo with 13-inch rotors from Galfer. The 19-inch front wheel is made from Carbon Fiber, so is the fender.

Bags are from Harley-Davidson, rear fender is from Curtis Hofmann.

The nice thing about overhauling your current bike is the money left to get a nice paint job.

125

The forks are genuine H-D, but with aftermarket Legends Axios cartridges.

the numbers – 120 horses and 120 Ft. Lbs of. torque – Chaz' was very satisfying.

Behind the motor is a stock, six-gear transmission, the two are connected by a stock primary chain from Harley Davidson and a clutch from Barnett. The final link is the stock belt to the rear wheel.

When it finally came time to paint all those body components, Chaz said, "It's a Harley, lets paint it black." And then Randy chimed in, "Give it a stripe." "Actually, it was Stephanie, my wife, who was the one to really came up with the complete color scheme," says Chaz, "she's the one who said the stripe should be white. Now we call it The Skunk."

Final assembly included a few final touches designed to give Chaz a ride that's fast and comfortable. Instead of the stock bars, Chaz bought ten-inch Modular bars and Contour grips from Ness. To ensure long rides are no-sweat, a Solo model seat from Danny Gray is combined with a pair of 18 inch Banana Boards.

When the bike was finished, someone asked Chaz, "How does it run?" The answer was short and to the point: "I love it. The ride is way better than a stock Harley, and it plants itself in corners extremely well."

Chaz's overhaul applied to the motor as well as the bike itself. Randy likes a displacement of 107 cubic inches, which is why he bored the cylinder to 3.937 and left the stroke alone. Randy ordered new pistons with 11.5 to 1 compression and a 58mm throttle body. The heads went to Rick Ward's shop for porting. In the end, the dyno recorded a top reading of 120 for both measurements.

Chapter 18

The Power of Suggestion

Tom Sperr runs a one-man shop. He does everything from building hot Dressers, to repairing a late model Harley that needs fluid changes and new brake pads. He lives and works in a small town in northern Minnesota, so it's not surprising that between Harley work he's been known to fix the exhaust on an old Ford pickup as a favor to one of the local neighbors.

Obviously, he's a mechanic who can do almost anything, including building the Performance Bagger seen here. It all started when Tom and a friend Rod were hanging out at a motorcycle event at Lake of the Ozarks. Rob was taken by some of the latest Baggers there, and Tom said, "We need to build one of those for you," and Rob replied, "Okay, I'll send you a new one."

Nothing like taking a brand-new Bagger and rip it apart and start all over. In this case, the owner wanted a certain motor displacement and a long list of aftermarket parts – and Tom Sperr is just the man to bring his wish to realty.

Primary chain is stock, the clutch is heavy duty. The final drive to the rear wheel is a chain (a MJK kit).

Rob Connolly is a big believer in the quality of MJK parts. Thus, the floorboards, shift lever and link to the transmission, carry that three-letter logo.

As promised, the new Road Glide was delivered to the shop with four miles on the odometer. Rod and Tom both agree that when the bike was done, the phrase Performance Bagger would fit this Harley-Davidson perfect. In fact, Performance is the first word in the two words that describe this new model from Harley-Davidson.

"Some of the bikes we saw at the event in the Ozark event had 143 motors," recalls Tom, "and I knew that Rob already had a 143 in his garage (a Twin Cam). So, there was no question as to how big I was going to build the motor."

When the 143 M-8 is pretty much done, there isn't much of the original mill left. Tom bought the big bore cylinders from Revolution Performance in Wisconsin, along with pistons; and a crank assembly with con-rods, from Darkhorse. The four and a half inch bores combined with a four and a half stroke gets you one 143 cubic inch V-twin – a displacement seldom seen in street bikes prior to the introduction of the M-8.

The mechanic who can do anything did the porting of the Harley heads in his shop and picked a Woods 6860 cam to motivate those new valves. The valve train wasn't complete to this V-Twin until Tom installed a set of roller rockers during the build. Feeding the ports and valves in the breathing department is a 64mm ported intake manifold and throttle body, from Rick Ward.

Until recently, a hot rod Harley meant a "built" motor, and maybe the builder changes out the primary and clutch. The rest of the typical two-wheeler stayed pretty much stock – the emphasis was the power, power, power. Now, the new Baggers get more than power - they get better suspension, brakes that stop on a dime, and a combination of handlebars, switches and controls, seat and floorboards. When one of these bikes is finished, there isn't too much of the origin bike left.

The big part of Rod's wish was a 143 cubic inch M-8. And to get enough horses Tom wanted to feed the M-8 enough air. Tom chose a 6860 camshaft from Woods – a cam that won the Daytona Dyno shoot out 11 years in a row. Tom did the porting of the heads and install a 64mm throttle body and a MJK air cleaner.

Up front it's a 17 inch wheel, manufactured (and colored) by MJK. Calipers and floating rotors have that same MJK logo.

At the request of Rob, Tom bought most of the components mentioned above from MJK. The MJK components don't come cheap, but they do have a certain look, and fans say they work as well as they look. Rob wanted MJK jewelry for the wheels and brakes, as well as items like floorboards, foot controls and handlebars.

The Mad Jap's wheels are the same size as stock (17 front and 16 rear) just a lot lighter and stronger than the Milwaukee units.

The front tire is a 130/60 x19; Dunlop Harley-Davidson D408F tire.

Available in color, Rob's are anodized in a blue that goes well with the factory's Zepher Blue. Each of the three calipers use four pistons, mated to the floating rotors that compliment those blue wheels.

Though the fork is stock, on the other end the shocks carry the Legend logo. Tom installed Revo-A models with a single spring, adjustable for preload; and a knob to adjust the rebound.

Per the current trend, Rob wanted new handlebars, and some tall risers. Both the bars and the risers are more components from MJK. Mounted to the bars is the factory master cylinders and mirrors. Bolted to the chassis are the controls and the floorboards from that same unique manufacturer.

At the end, Rob got exactly what he wanted. A new Bagger with a 200-horse motor and all the latest and most advanced components. A custom machine that can sit proudly with any other Performance Bagger at any event.

Hard to see, the rear brakes are MJK caliper and rotor. Rear tire is 180/65 x 16; Dunlop Harley-Davidson D407T. Rear shocks are Revo-As.

Chapter 19

More than a Performance Bagger

by Paul Yaffe

The Road Glide seen here has lived more than one life. Initially, the 2019 model was purchased and customized for shows. Like a model dressed in the latest at Fashion Week, the Glide rolled into shows and events wearing the latest components from Paul Yaffe. The COVID plague, however, got in the way of that career. "Everything shut down, no more rallies." recalls Paul. "We closed our show room and locked the door. No T-shirts on the wall and no displays filled with motorcycle-jewelry. All that empty space became my shop. Right about then is when our minds started turning towards performance components. Performance was getting traction and I got on the movement. We wanted to do performance bikes, which I like that stuff anyway. And one of the first things I did was order and install a 131-inch motor from the local Harley-Davidson dealer for the 2019 Road Glide."

"Once I got the bike running and used it for some rides," said Paul, "I liked the 131, but I wanted more. So, we installed a more aggressive 465 cam from Feul and ported the heads. Along the porting, we added a

Not your standard Performance Bagger, Yaffe's Golden Rule evolved through the years. With each generation it became more modern - the latest aftermarket parts are the very current items - the neck was cut off the Golden Rule and reinstalled, the Big Wheel kit was also part of the SRT kit. Last but not least, the fast H-D crate motor became a whole lot faster. Studio photos by: Olivier Touron.

The tank is decorated with the Dimple Die Dash kit.

There are abundant gas tanks with knee recesses, but this one stands out due to the way it's finished with the soft corners at the top and bottom.

H-D SE 64mm throttle body with high-flow injectors. Once on the dyno we did our tuning – one of the things we did was made our own two-into-one exhaust. The new parts and the tuning gave us about another 30 or more horses and 40 more-foot pounds of torque – and boy, that work we did really wake up that motor. The bike felt like it was shot out of a canon."

Considering the added horses, it's perhaps surprising that the driveline is mostly stock. In the primary cavity there's a one-piece compensator from Darkhorse, and an AIM Race lock-up clutch assembly. Other than that, Paul left the tranny and driveline stock, explaining, "I've broken belts in my life, but I don't do burn-outs and I haven't broken a belt on this bike."

A rider who likes to twist the throttle on a bike with too much horsepower needs good aftermarket suspension and brakes. The overhaul of the suspension on this ride is not the same recipe used by most of the riders and builders. Paul didn't just install an inverted fork assembly on the bike. No, he started by cutting off the neck - an essential step to installing the SRT kit - you might call it Paul Yaffe's big-wheel kit.

The basic components in the kit include a 20x5.5-inch front wheel, a tire made specifically for the kit, the machined spacer that pushes the neck out, wider triple trees (with 7 degrees of rake in addition of the 7 inched in the factory neck), a fender, axle, and spacers for the fender and the ABS.

Paul is proud of his SRT kit and thinks it's one of the best. "We measured the trail in the stock Baggers and those stock Baggers have 6 1/2 inches of positive trail. We made sure when we designed our kit, and install the kit, that the bike has the same 6 1/2 inches of positive trail. We're not changing anything from the factory-designed balance and the way the wheels work together to control the vehicle, which is super important."

A fender comes with the kit, but for this bike Paul used a SRT Café front fender. The kit includes a fairing bracket as well, necessary to keep the fairing positioned correctly after the neck is moved. Fork legs do not come with the kit, but do come with spacers so the stock fork legs can be used with the kit. For this project they used Gold/Black Anodized DC Inverted SRT fork legs. The rest of the suspension modifying includes a pair of 13 inches of ODC remote Reservoir Race Shocks.

The 20 x 5.5-inch front wheel is a "Bandit" wheel paired to a Shinko 777-81H SRT performance tire. The rear 18-inch rear wheel just happens to match the Bandit front wheel, wrapped with a Shinko 180/55 performance tire, and both wheels are gold anodized. Slowing that big front wheel is a Rebuffini Radial Race Caliper (gold anodized of course) and a 15-inch jagged floating rotor. In back, a Brembo caliper was chosen to squeeze that rotor.

The fender in back is a Bagger Nation "SS" Short Sport Rear Fender, with the BN Tri-Pod Lights. In between the two fenders is the seat, and a gas tank with recesses on the sides to allow the rider to tuck in his or her knees. The cut-outs on this bike are different than most, in that the cut-out from one side, became the new concave patch in the other side – with a little massaging. The finished tank is a slippery shape like no others. On top of the tank is the Bagger Nation Dimple Die Dash Kit. Behind the tank is a Le Pera Black Daytona II seat with Gold Double Diamond stitching and deluxe passenger backrest.

The bags are stock units from Harley, with no stretches, because you don't want the bottom of the deep bags dragging on a sharp turn with a good rider. In front of the bags, however, is the BN Swoop, a concave side cover that helps the bags blend with the rest of the bike.

There's no doubt that this is one kick-ass Bagger. Big motor, lots of horsepower, suspension and brakes that are state of the art. What about the aesthetics? Rolling Art Custom Motorcycle Paint started with Mazda RED paint, and horizontal panels in white with streaks of red outlined in gold. And black

Hard to create something that's truly unique. Try a 3-D windshield carved from a solid piece of aluminum on hours of CNC – then gold anodized.

Nothing but the best, a Le Pera Black Daytona II seat with gold double diamond stitching.

Note the shift arm and the stealth heel shift lever on the other end. Floorboards from Rubuffini.

The handlebars are another Yaffe well-known part, the Monkey Sport Bars with a clamp-area that works for either 1, or 1-1/4-inch clamp area.

borders between the red and white. The frosting on this cake is the windshield cut from a billet of aluminum and then anodized in gold to match the wheels.

When the Golden Rule was turned loose on the street, it turned out to be both a good day-to-day ride in traffic, and a rocket when necessary. There were no surprises in the handlings or the motor. Paul did test the rocket side of the Golden Rule on highway 10 as he headed home in Phoenix one day. "There wasn't much traffic and I come up on a couple of guys in front of me," recalls Paul. "One in a Mustang 5.0 and another in a Challenger. They were goofing around with each other; you could hear them revving their engines and teasing each other."

"I pulled up next to them and I was like, come on let's go, that kind of thing. They took off, so I dropped a gear, tucked in and rolled into it. I had that thing wide open, and it hit 147. I'd never gone that fast. I had it on the GPS screen not the speedo. I was doing 147 and I held it there for 60-plus seconds. A minute and a half, that's a long time when you're going that fast."

Right out of the catalog – Short Sport rear fender, Tri-Pod Lightning Bolts, and "Bagserts" on the Bagger hinge cover inserts.

The master cylinder is from Rubuffini, Race Controls all the way from Italy. Foot boards and pegs from the same company.

The front wheel measures 20 inches – a SRT Front Wheel (gold anodized) from Yaffe. The front caliper is Rebuffini Radial Race Caliper (Gold also) and a jagged floating rotor.

Installing the 131 Crate Motor from H-D made the bike faster, but not fast enough – Paul and crew focused on breathing, from the heads to the exhaust – then it really was fast.

Chapter 20

You Have to Look Twice

Mark Foff looks like the typical rider with a typical Bagger – as long as you don't look too closely. If you take a close look at the bike, and talk to the owner, you'll understand; this ain't no stock Bagger with a typical owner.

Racing on the street is illegal and so is gambling. Mark does both. "Those guys down south, they like to race and they like to gamble," he explains. "Sometimes I go out with Kendall Johnson and friends, we go and find the serious guys, and set up a series of races. So far, I've lost only one race, and my biggest win was ten thousand dollars."

To win all those races you need a damned-strong motor. The sleeping motorcycle started life as a 2018 M-8 Bagger with a 114 cubic inch V-twin. Currently, it's a 143-inch monster, thanks to V TWIN POWERSPORTS in Chicago, Illinois. Once they had the motor opened up, V TWIN crew installed a 4.5-inch stroke crankshaft,

Generally, looking at the left side of a white Bagger is boring, a waste of time. With Mark's Bagger, if you're a motorhead, slow down as you walk past, it's worth your time.

assembled from S&S components and balanced by Darkhorse. For cylinders, V TWIN started with Harley-Davidson cylinders which they bored first. Next, they installed their liner and did the final honing to fit the eleven-to-one Corrillo pistons (designed by V TWIN) connected with the crankshaft with Corrillo rods. A 4.5 stroke and a 4.5-inch bore makes for a square 143 cubic inch V-Twin. The heads are another V TWIN product.

To make sure the white whale can win against all those bikes, Mark needed more than just abundant cubic inches and great tuning. He and V-TWIN decided the answer was a blower from Pro Charger. The actual blower is mounted on the left side. The air goes through the blower then crosses to the other side through the plumbing, then it passes through the intercooler. Finally, through the air filter and the V TWIN 65mm throttle body, where the air picks up the mist of gas from the 1300cc injectors.

The result of all that machinery installed by a skilled crew, created a motor with a boost of 19 pounds, and 300-plus horsepower.

There are a few of what you might call accessories.

With a blower-bike, most of the machinery is on the left side – the drive, the blower itself and the crossover (and an air-shifter) …

… that delivers the pressured air to the intercooler and then the 65mm throttle body. Once through the throttle body it's to the heads, ported by V TWIN.

First, there's an air-shifter. Second, is the Max CU 2 computer system. The computer controls the fuel and spark maps – so if the juice isn't primo race fuel, Mark can use a map that works for the local fuel.

Getting 300 plus horses to the rear tire – without breaking any one of various stock drive-line components – means a drivetrain made up of heavy duty parts. Between the motor and the transmission there's the double factory chain (factory), with a billet compensator on one end and a V-TWIN clutch basket on the other, (filled with steel and fiber discs). Next in line is the transmission, and of course the teams chose a Grudge Box from Baker.

Next is a V TWIN kit to convert belt to chain-drive, with a 530-chain driving a 17X5.5 inch wheel wrapped by a Shinko drag tire. Supporting that wheel and drag-tire is a Plus-4 Swingarm from A-1 Cycle. 130/60/19 Metzeler tire with rotors from Galfer squeezed by the stock, four-piston calipers. Both wheels from Brock's are manufactured from Carbon Fiber – proof those Carbon wheels really are tough.

When Mark built a new knew bike, he knew what he wanted - and what he didn't. The sheet metal and paint were installed in Milwaukee, no crazy paint jobs. The same goes for the handlebars and controls. The suspension is from that same shop – though Mark did improve the suspension up front with cartridges and shocks with reservoir gas reservoir to support the swingarm.

Mark spent enough money to create a second bike. Instead, he got a long list of races he won, a pocket full of money, and only one loss. Mark thinks all that money was well spent.

The boring white Bagger parked on the illegal drag strip – a totally appropriate place for Mark's 300 horsepower Drag-Bagger.

The Man of the Hour

There's one man who built at least three bikes in this book, and dozens of others. A skilled bike builder who simply isn't known to a lot of people.

Randy Cramer is that man. It started back in 1983 when he moved to Spearfish to run a Honda Motorcycle Service Department. Three years later he switched to working on cars. As Randy tells it, "I'm not afraid to wrench on nearly anything. I don't care if it's a farm tractor, a D-8 Cat, or a motorcycle, it's all nuts and nuts. But what I really like is Harleys."

Not a person to sit, by June of 2006 it was time to open his own shop. As Randy recalls the new shop, "Once I had my shop (Dakota V-Twin), I started working on Harleys right away."

Then and now, Randy works mostly by himself, with an occasionally helper to help run the front-end. You would think Randy would have his own special Harley and he does. Randy's ride is a Dyna with a Randy-special-107 Twin Cam motor with a FXRT fairing up front and a pair of Beetle bags on the back.

You might think Randy spends all his time in the shop building hot rod Harleys, but as mentioned earlier he can fix almost anything. "I do build bikes full time - in winter," explains Randy. "In the summer I do mostly day-to-day maintenance. Eighty percent of the maintenance customers are local and the rest are tourists. The tourists that come in once, almost always become good customers. They stop in whenever they're in town."

Whether it's an overhaul or an oil change, customers know Randy will do it right. That's how he's worked for life. And his true reward is a long list of regular customers.

Above:
At home in the shop and on his personal ride –
a Dyna with a 107 cubic inch Twin Cam
(Randy's favorite displacement), a RT fairing, bags from
Corbin and a flawless black paint job.

Left:
The hands and the smile of a
hard-working Harley mechanic.

Wolfgang and Timothy Remus have a variety of books. Find your favorite at: www.barnesandnoble.com www.amazon.com

Titles	ISBN
Advanced Custom Motorcycle Assembly & Fabrication	9781929133239
Advanced Custom Motorcycle Wiring- Revised Edition	9781935828761
Advanced Custom Painting Techniques	9781929133147
Advanced Pinstripe Art	9781929133321
Advanced Sheet Metal Fabrication	9781929133697
Advances Tattoo Art - Revised	9781935828822
Airbrush Bible	9781929133864
Airbrushing with Vince Goodeve:	
How to Airbrush 2 and 4 wheel Hot Rods	9781941064368
Body Painting	9781929133666
Building Hot Rods	9781929133437
Composite Materials Fabrication Handbook #2	9781929133932
Composite Materials: Fabrication Handbook #1	9781929133765
Composite Materials: Fabrication Handbook #3	9781935828662
Composite Materials: Step-By-Step Projects	9781929133369
Custom Bike Building Basics:	
Tips and Tricks for the Backyard Garage Mechanic	9781935828624
Custom Motorcycle Fabrication:	
Materials, Welding, Lathe & Mill Work, Chassis Assembly	9781941064467
Custom Motorcycle Fabrication:	
Materials, Welding, Mill and Lathe, Frame Construction	9781935828792
Enthusiasts Guide: Honda Motorcycles 1959-1985	9781935828853
Harley-Davidson Evo, Hop-Up & Rebuild Manual	9781941064337
Harley-Davidson FXR Bible	9781941064559
Harley-Davidson Twin Cam: Hop-Up & Rebuild Manual	9781929133697

Titles	ISBN
Honda 70 Enthusiast's Guide: All CL, CT, SL, & XL 72cc models 1969-1994	9781941064351
Honda Mini Trail	9781941064320
Honda Motorcycles 1959-1985	9781941064481
Hot Rod Wiring: A Detailed How-To Guide	9781929133987
How to Airbrush Pin-Ups	9781929133802
How to Build a Cheap Chopper	9781929133178
How to Build a Chopper	9781929133062
How to Build an Old Skool Bobber: Build Your Own Bobber or Chopper	9781935828006
How to Fix American V-Twin Motorcycles	9781929133727
How to Paint Tractors & Trucks	9781929133475
How-To Airbrush, Pinstripe & Goldleaf	9781935828693
How-To Chop Tops	9781929133499
Kosmoski's New Kustom Painting Secrets	9781929133833
Learning the English Wheel	9781935828891
Power Hammers	9781929133604
Sheet Metal Bible	9781929133901
Sheet Metal Fab Basics	9781929133468
So Cal Speed Shop's How to Build Hot Rod Chassis	9781941064047
Sportster/Buell Engine Hop-Up Guide: Harley-Davidson	9781929133093
Tecnicas Avanzadas de Pintura a Medida	9781929133277
Tattoo Bible Book Three - Soft Cover	9781935828754
Tattoo Bible Book Two - Soft Cover	9781929133857
Tattoo Bible One - Soft Cover	9781929133840
Tattoo Models	9781941064689
Triumph Motorcycle Restoration	9781941064276
Triumph Motorcycle Restoration: Pre-Unit	9781929133635
Triumph Motorcycle Restoration - Unit Motors	9781929133420
Ultimate Sheet Metal Fabrication	9780964135895
Vintage Dirt Bikes: Enthusiasts Guide	9781929133314

www.ingramcontent.com/pod-product-compliance
Lightning Source LLC
Chambersburg PA
CBHW061212230426
43665CB00032B/2990